# KNOW THE SEERS OF INDIA

## (*A collection of One Act plays on Sages and Devotees of ancient India*)

# Dr. C. D. Verma

# Contents

# PREFACE

The *Rishis*, qua the seers, of ancient India represent a rich socio-cultural and religio-spiritual heritage of the Hindus. The sages may be remote in time, but they are not remote in thought. Since the human nature is immutable, therefore our seers are relevant to all times. They disclose the working of the primal impulses of the human soul, cutting across the differences of race and geographical boundaries. Before dilating on the most exacting subject of the Indian *Rishis*, it is pertinent to ask: "who is a *Rishi.?*" A *Rishi* is one who has "*Drishti,*" who has the vision to envision time past, time present and time future. Since he has the discerning eye, he can see the "unseen," the "unforeseen." Therefore, by a natural corollary, he is a "seer." In fact, through arduous *tapasya* (penance), he acquires a "celestial" vision, an "I" which brings him closer to the dictum "*Aham Brahmasmi,*" or "*so'uhm,*" ("I am HE"). Further, the definition and meaning of the word "sage" also accentuates the same aphorism, for a sage means a saint who is sagacious, who is replete with wisdom, and who is perceptive and prudent. And what the *Rishis*, or the seers, were able to see through their intuitive knowledge, were the *Vedas*. The word *Veda* is derived from the root "vedi," which means "divine knowledge," an illimitable store-house of education, an inexhaustible mine of the profoundest wisdom -- spiritual, secular and temporal -needed by mankind. And India is lucky to have a compilation of such "revealed knowledge," in the form of the *Vedas*, for the *Vedas*, in fact, are the compilation of hymns by various sages. But banefully we have forgotten this ancient *vedic* lore, our valued inheritance, after spurning it as mysticism. And down the ages we have become oblivious of our *Rishis*, of our seers and saints. In this book an attempt has been made to retrieve the leaned sages from the hoary past to bring them closer to the present generation. Some of us may have heard the names of some *Rishis*, but perhaps they may not be knowing much about them. Therefore, an effort has been made to cull from the *vedic*, post-*vedic* scriptures and the classical literature, the *Ramayana* and the *Mahabharata*, the legends and myths appertaining the seers, their births, parents, family, their actions and reactions, and so on. For an ordinary reader it is not easy to comprehend the complexities of the lives and deeds of the *Rishis*. Therefore, all those legends and stories that relate to the sages, and are essential for understanding an intricate subject, have been rendered in the dramatic form in "One-Act" plays. Thus, this book becomes a collection of One-Act plays on *Rishis*. Some devotees, such as Dhruva, Prahlada, Shabri, hitherto known, yet not known much, have also been included. And also included is a satire on Yudhishtra, that if he opts to contest an election in the present day Bharata, what would happen to him. In fact, many years ago, I had read a story on this subject in a Hindi paper, which provided me an inspiration to rehash it into a One-Act play in my own way.

A novel device has been adopted in this collection of One-Act plays. I have introduced a narrator, named Gunadhya. The narrator's function is to comment on the personality of the seers. He sees what we fail to see. He follows clues to solve the mysteries encompassing the sages, and provides much of interesting information. He makes the task of this author easy in ways more than one. And also enhances the interest of the readers.

Normally, an author looks for some renowned scholar, critic, or author for writing a "Foreword." But I decided to discard that practice. I requested my two daughters, Dr. Manjula Batra, and Dr. Seema Sharma, both academicians and creative writers, to pen the Forewords. And they did so extremely well. Dr. Manjula Batra has already published a unique book, *The Peacock Plume: Nar and Narayan*. In this book she has versified some selected episodes of the *Mahabharata* and the *Gita*. Similarly, Dr Seema Sharma, has also brought out a collection of her poems.

I am grateful to my learned daughters to help me prepare this book. They read the entire manuscript and gave me useful suggestions which I incorporated in the book.

I am also grateful to the publishers for their cooperation to bring out this book in an elegant form.

**Dr. C. D. VERMA**
Former Associate professor and Head,
Department of English,
Hans Raj College,
University of Delhi.

# FOREWORD: ONE

*If inspiration is the root of poetry, it is related to ecstasy.*

**-*SOCRATES***

An inspired work of art, indeed, is this erudite anthology of plays by my scholarly father, Dr C. D. Verma. Only the purest, noblest and most elevated human beings embark upon such a quest. A seer literally means 'one with insight to see, to seek the truth'. A poet is a seer, a figure divinely inspired as he becomes one with Brahma, the creator. **'Kavir Manishi Paribhu Swaymbhu'** so propound our ancient Sanskrit texts. Verily, this book creates a virtual vision of a **Tapovana** (a forest of austerities) where Gunadhya, the narrator, seems to bring alive the intriguing world of sages and seers from the Vedas, Puranas and the Upanishads, taking us away from '**The world (that) is too much with us'** as Wordsworth sang.

The prologue of each play triggers the imagination of readers, laying the foundation of what is to follow. The curtain-raiser by Gunadhya is a soliloquy establishing a rapport between the narrator and the audience, creating a seamless woof and warp of the narrative. I'm reminded of Marlow, the narrator of Conrad in his novels **The Heart of Darkness**, **Lord Jim** and others. The well-structured, short scenes lend a smooth unobstructed flow to the main events. In this ground-breaking work, the author explores how the saints, born in *Vedic* Era, left for us the spiritual heritage of sublime teachings that has pervaded the human psyche so much so that the pristine essence still echoes in the air through socio-religious practices. Each word of the sacred **Gayatri Mantra** by Rishi Vishvamitra and **Maha Mrityunjay Mantra** by Rishi Markandeya, the mantras which are believed to destroy all sins and purge the souls, has been beautifully explained by the author.

One cannot enjoy a drama in the absence of *rasa or the quintessence* that is the vital element of a drama. *Rasas* are created by *bhavas,* the state of mind. God himself is *Rasa* **"Raso Vai Sah"**. That is why the tales of saints in dramatic form evoke emotions through *rasa,* in one or the other form. The celestial voice in the mesmerizing sagas of sages like Rishyashringa, Ashtavakra, Vasishtha, Gautama, Shabri, Bharadwaja, Vishwamitra, hails one to enter into the consciousness of each saint, discovering the ultimate Truth of being and becoming, elevating the ephemeral *Nar* into the Supreme Godhead *Narayana.* As ever, Dr Verma's insight and analytical faculties come into play hitherto, evoking the varied emotions through his dramatic art: awe, horror, piety, ecstasy, fear, tranquility, and so on. Dhruv's steadfast devotion makes one ecstatic, Dhadichi's sacrifice for a greater cause elicits piety, whereas Bharadwaja, standing tall amongst all the sages of ancient India, evokes awe. While the tale of Rishi Matang and Shabri fills the heart with compassion and reverence, even as it gives a socio-political message of 'Karma'. Ashtavakra becomes an archetypal symbol of supremacy of mind over matter, creating horror and piety in turns; Vishvamitra embodies the concept of *nirvana* through relinquishing ego. A lofty moral, a profound philosophy, a sublime emotion or *Rasa,* that is what defines each play.

Plato contended that a dramatist achieves his purpose when he successfully elevates and evokes emotions in the audience who end up losing their sense of moderation. Aristotle argued: 'A drama does generate emotions of pity and terror.' The Greeks maintained that a poet was a "Vates" (Prophet, poet, seer), an inspired prophet. A strong connection was presupposed between literature and truth, poetry and divinity. The convention of the invocation is a sign of such a supposition. This work by Dr. C.D. Verma bears witness to the Greek theory.

This book is an attempt to discover the role and

contribution of a galaxy of saints and seers who shaped not only the religious-cultural way of Indian life over several centuries, but also contributed to the geographical outlook of Bharat. They all transcended the temporal barriers through ascetic practices and provided a solid ethical landscape to people. For instance, Kashyapa, a revered Vedic sage of Hinduism, one of the *Saptarishis* (the seven ancient sages of the **Rigveda)**, became the founder of Kashmir. According to Christopher Snedden, the name Kashmir could have been a shortened form of "Kashyapa Mir", or "the lake of the sage Kashyapa'. It could also have been derived from the term "Kashyapa Meru", which means the sacred mountains of Kashyapa. Saint Agastya, as depicted in the **Ramayana,** went South when Shiva asked him to go there and restore the balance of the earth, for the weight of Agastya was equal to the weight of all the other *Rishis* put together. Agastya is renowned in the South as the father of Siddha, the southern form of Ayurveda. He is also associated with occult arts of architecture and forecasting as well as formulation of the Tamil language. Even today a mountain peak between Tamil Nadu and Kerala associated with rare medicinal herbs is called *Agastyamalai,* a reminder of his presence in and contribution to civilization in South India. So, much impact of saints on different parts of India can be seen. These dramas aim at educating our youth about the Vedic India and our rich cultural history. For the *Saptrishis* are regarded in the *Vedas* as the patriarchs of the Vedic religion. We are all considered descendants of some or the other saint.

The author, by dramatizing the tales of each of the major sages, seers and rishis, goes beyond the narrative and looks for the eternal, seeking to find the cause of all cause, the Supreme Being and endeavours to connect. And one who finally gets connected is a veritable saint.

My best wishes to Dr Verma for the success of this grand creation! Hope it brings as much Light to every reader as it did to me.

**Dr Manjula Batra**
Associate professor and Head,
Department of English,
S.D. College, Palwal

# FOREWORD: TWO

I feel proud to write a foreword for the book *Know the Seers of India: A Collection of One act plays on Sages and Devotees of ancient India* authored by Dr. C.D. Verma, a versatile scholar in the field of English literature, with the credit of having written around 50 books. Being born to him as a daughter, I have always seen him giving references from the Vedic Myths and characters to take a cue from and deal with any situation in our life. If one is allowed to write about his credentials, it will become a book by itself. His insight and experience merging so well with his store of knowledge and wisdom, offers a ground to the readers for more exploration on the rich *Vedic* literature.

The book in your hands is a compilation of one act plays on the great seers and devotees of India. It was contemplated by Dr. Verma in order to develop an exhaustive understanding of the various aspects of the purpose of their birth in connection with the spatio-temporal immensity of the universe and the reincarnation of God Vishnu. His curiosity to explore the *raison d'etre* of the *rishis* in a particular period and dynasty, got manifested in the form of a dramatic representation of the primordial reality hidden in their causal tendencies and effects thereof. Each story is dramatically narrated by Gunadhya, a celestial being, the narrator of tales in Somdeva's famous book *Kathasaritasagara*, that is the Ocean of Stories. The deliberate selection of Gunadhya as narrator makes the narration spiritually inclined reminding one of Sanjaya narrating the action in the climactic battle of Kurukshetra to his blind king Dhritrashtra. This idea of making a virtuous being narrate a story signifies the predominance of intuitive knowledge over material blindness.

The author authentically delineates the ancient myths and origin of some most powerful *Mantras* emanating from the mouths of those divine souls to lead humanity. *Rishi* Vishwamitra uttered a few words of wisdom that were later included in *The Rigveda* as the **'Gayatri Mantra'** and *Rishi* Markandeya gave the **'Maha Mrityunjaya Mantra'** as a healing force for all temporal and spiritual ailments, which also found its place in *The Rig veda, Yajur veda* and *Atharva veda.* Seers are the human beings of highest vibrations who can see beyond what a human eye can see, irrespective of time and space. Dr. Verma's choice of the very subject of legends related to the life and actions of the renowned sages and devotees, advocates his wish to lay down the spiritual and moral significance of this book. The dramatic version of these stories makes it easier for the youth of today to get absorbed in. Presenting Yuddhishtra and Duryodhana in a modern context triggers many ethical issues of the electoral Mahabharata of the political world. Each played his *'chal'* (move) on the *'chauser'*(electoral dice-board) to prove his right to the candidature in the upcoming elections.

Each play culminates with an epilogue as a conscious effort of the author to relate the respective legend to the complexities of our contemporary society and its ethos. The bases of all these legends are *The Gita, Puranas, Upanishadas* and other *Vedic* texts which he quotes at relevant places in the plays. This book takes us to the India of ancient times, when it was inhabited by sages and saints, devotees, demi-gods and even *apsaras* like Menaka, Urvashi, Rambha who could travel to and from Heavens on a mission to establish order on earth. The stories of the birth of *Rishya-Shringa* (man with horns) or *Varaha* (boar), the incarnation of God Vishnu or the divine cow of *Rishi Vashishta* were no fairy-tales. If the **Gayatri Mantra** exists today, so did its creator. If the festival of Holi is celebrated in the honour of the great devotee Prahlad and the burning of his aunt Holika, so he must have lived sometime on earth. Each legend conveys a message of victory of *Dharma* over *Adharma,* which is subtly interpreted by the author.

The present book is a welcome introduction to the mythical world of the *Vedic* and *Puranic* legends inspiring the readers to follow the path of righteousness and virtues. It will usher the readers into a new realm of devotional and spiritual journey to seek communion with the Supreme soul, *Parmatma.* I pray that this narrative wisdom by Dr. Verma leads all its readers to understand the theory of **Karma** and the message of the Universal good - **Sarve bhavantu sukhinaḥ**, as the crux of the Indian philosophy. My best wishes to my father to reach a huge readership again though this work of scholarship!

**Dr. Seema Sharma**
Poet/Writer/Editor
Principal, HES-II

# INTRODUCTION

Our desire to go to the mountains never wanes. They have always fascinated and lured us as abodes of gods, sages and seers. Mount Kailash has been the abode of Lord Shiva, as also of Kubera, the god of wealth. It was at Mount Kailash that sage Parashu-rama was refused to meet Shiva, which incident resulted in a brawl between Ganesha and the sage, and Parashu-rama severed one of the tusks of Ganesha. Since then, Ganesha is called *Eka-Danta*. On Mount Meru is situated the heaven of Lord Indra, and the cities of celestial beings. Mount Olympus has been the residence of Greek gods. Lord Christ delivered the Sermon on the Mount.

The holy shrines of Lord Vishnu at Badrinath, and of Lord Shiva at Kedarnath, are situated on the top of mountains. And so is the shrine of goddess Vaishno Devi at Katra (Jammu). Chitrakuta has been the seat of *Rishi* Balmiki's hermitage, where Lord Rama and Sita found refuge at different times. And Parashu-rama, the *Chiranjeevi* saint, has his abode at Mahindergiri mountain. Obviously, mountains represent elevation, and the communion of the blessed. Saints and hermits invariably chose mountains for meditation and *tapasya* (penance), for on mountains reign peace and tranquility. Therefore, mountains have always beckoned us to undertake pilgrimages to the holy shrines. Like most of you, I too have responded to the call of mountains umpteen times in my life. I have been to Badrinath and Kedarnath shrines four times. My first visit to these shrines was more than two decades ago, when I embarked on a temporal journey as a tourist. A tourist is "one who makes a tour for pleasure or recreation. "While a pilgrim is one who travels to a holy place, qua shrine, as a devotee. I went to Badrinath and Kedarnath as a tourist, but returned as a pilgrim. Something out-of-the-ordinary happened which metamorphosed me from a tourist to a pilgrim. The rendezvous became my first contact with the "spiritual India," India of seers, saints and gods.

On my way back from Badrinath, I was thrilled by nature's splendour with Alaknanda gurgling out of glaciers, serpentinely speeding through the gorges, lapping upon and over the boulders, tumultuous, majestic and awe-inspiring. After staying for the night at Nandprayag, situated at the confluence of the roaring Alaknanda and rumbling Mandakini, I took a detour from Karan Prayag to Nainital via Ranikhet. After passing through valley glades full of fruit orchards, reverberating with birds warbling their different notes and the susurrus of a small stream flowing through them, I reached Bhowali in the afternoon. Bhowali is a small hill resort, situated equidistance from Nainital and Bhimtal: the trio are the favourite haunt of the tourists.

At Bhowali, my wife, a spiritually-inclined devout woman, told me that she had visited Nainital and Bhimtal several times. She insisted on visiting Kal Bhairava shrine at Ghora Khal, situated about three kilometers from Bhowali on the Bhowali-Bhimtal road. She was told about this shrine by a close friend who had been a regular visitor to this place.

When we reached the Ghora-Khal temple, perched among tall pine trees at an altitude higher than that of Bhowali, or Nainital, we were amazed at out-of-the-ordinary, exceptionally rare spectacle. There were bells and bells, hundreds of bells, thousands of bells; God knows how many, hung all around, everywhere, wherever the space was there. It was a romantic setting among sylvan surroundings, which engendered a mystic spell replete with holy dread at the Kal Bhairava shrine. Such a large number of bells, I had never seen before. The enchanting ambience wrought a change in my mood from a tourist to that of a pilgrim. It was a culmination of my experience which had started at Badrinath.

Ghora Khal derives its name from "khal," that is a water -course, or a watering place for the horses (of the Nawab of Rampur). Once upon a time Ghora Khal and Bhowali formed a part of the erstwhile Rampur state. The Head priest told me that the bells were hung by the devotees after their wishes were fulfilled by Kal Bhairava, the presiding deity of the temple. Bhairava is a deity which figures in the Hindu, Buddhist and Jain mythology, tradition and iconography. He is believed to have been born of Lord Shiva's blood, and is a particularly fierce form of Lord shiva. Kal Bhairava, worshipped by the Hindus, wears a little girdle with small bells on its waist. Since he carries bells on his waist, hence the offerings of bells.

Recalling the history and the folk- legend, the Head Priest informed that it was in 1911 that his father had joined the service of General H. Wheeler, who owned the property of Ghora Khal. At that time, the Bhairava temple, popularly called in local parlance as "Gola Divaya," existed. The temple derives its name from Golu or Gola Baba, a revered seer, believed to be an incarnation of Lord Bhairava.

Annoyed at the bellowing of the conch shells and the ringing of the bells, General Wheeler ordered his men to demolish the temple. But when his men went there to perform the errand, they could not locate the temple. At night General Wheeler had hallucinations and saw illusions, as if his bed was moving up and down in circles among the jingle of utensils. Awed by the supernatural happenings, he is said to have visited the temple the next morning and offered a 15 kg bell as a mark of his obeisance and expiation to the deity. The bell is still hung there. He also sanctioned a grant of Rs. 15 per month (a big amount then) for the upkeep of the temple.

Yet another legend has it that Raja Jhala Rai of Kumaon had seven wives. But he had no issue to succeed him on the throne. He was advised to worship Lord Bhairava to propitiate him, which he did. Pleased with the king's devotion, Lord Bhairavaa, one day, appeared in his dreams, and told him that he himself will take birth in his house provided he married for the eighth time.

One day Raja Jhala Rai, on a hunting expedition, reached a dense forest. He came to a small rivulet to quench his thirst. As he was about to drink water, a young damsel suddenly appeared and said that before he drank water, he should do a good deed, and disengage the two fighting bulls. The king, known for his valour, did his best but could not separate the bulls. However, the lady disengaged the fighting bulls with her bare hands. This impressed the king, who proposed marriage to her. Eventually, king Jhala Rai married the lady, named Kalinga.

With the passage of time, Kalinga conceived and gave birth to a son. The eldest queens, out of jealousy, replaced the baby-boy with a stone, and threw the newly-born child into the river. It was, however, rescued by a fisherman, who brought him up. When the child grew up, he made a wooden horse and rode to the place where his step-mothers were bathing. The boy asked them to clear the way as his horse wanted to drink water. The women laughed at him and asked: "How can a wooden horse drink water?" The boy retorted that if a wooden horse could not drink water, how could a woman give birth to a stone?

The king came to know of the wrong the elder queens had done to the youngest one. He ordered the women to be hanged. But the boy intervened and saved the lives of his queen-mothers. Later King Jhala Rai enthroned his son as the king in his place. Since then, he has been worshipped as the incarnation of Bhairava at Ghora Khal, where a statue of a young man riding a white horse is installed. This was my first tryst with the Spiritual India.

I know that the agnostics will not believe the tale narrated above. They will simply label it as superstition, as an old wife's tale sans credibility. Nevertheless, the legend aforementioned is for those who walk by faith, and who believe in the Biblical quote: "Faith is the force of life." Those who have faith in religious India will appreciate the fact that the bells were hung all over the precincts of the temple by those whose wishes were fulfilled by the presiding deity. The devotees throng the Kal Bhairava temple, day in and day out, supplicate to the presiding god, and when their wishes are fulfilled by the blessings of Bhairava, they hang bells as manifestation of their gratitude.

There is no denying the fact that how-so-ever modern one may become, the primitive man in him, having faith in myths, rituals and rites, has the tendency to repeat himself. A myth is a spoken correlation of rite, a simple primordial proto-science effort of the imagination to identify the human with the non-human world, the most typical result of which is a story weaved around a god. An example of this dictum is in evidence at the Ghora Khal temple of considerable antiquity. Obviously, myths, legends, rituals live on the outskirts of civilization.

The fact remains that we, the Hindus, are *Rishi santan* (progeny of sages). *Rishis* of ancient India are our ancestors, our forefathers. The lineage of each Hindu family goes back to one or the other *Rishi*. This fact stands substantiated by sub-castes, qua surnames, such as Bharadwaja, Kashyap, Vashisht, Parashar, Shandilya, and so on. In fact, the progenies of the *Rishis* are known by *Gotras,* such as Bharadwaja, Gautama, Kashyap, Parashar etc. We are all descendants of *Rishis*.

As a Rigvedic term, *Gotra* simply means "cow pen," or "herd of cows." The specific meaning being "family lineage kin" (as it were herd within an enclosure). No socio-religious ritual, or rite, such as marriage, child-birth, *mundan*, *Shraddha* rites, is complete without invoking the *Gotra* of the family. Verily, *Gotra* identifies us with the past, with the sages of India.

Down the years, between the past and the present, things have taken a down turn. Today, a family is just an urbanized, sanitized individualistic generation, oblivious of its roots and in quest of identity. For such families, or individuals in the world, who are in search of their past, their roots, their identity, there is one age-old institution in India, an amazing one, a singular example of its kind in the world, which satisfies the subliminal urges (existing or functioning below the threshold of conscious awareness), and helps the atomized individualistic generation to rediscover the roots lost. They are the *Pandas* (family priests) at Hardwar, the record holders of the family trees of pilgrims. They bring people together in time past and time present, in space divided by thousands of miles.

As soon as a pilgrim arrives in Hardwar for any religious rite, *mundan*, or for the immersion of ashes of his dead kith and kin, he would be approached by a Panda. Here is a chronicle of my personal experience, which can be your experience too. As soon as I parked my car in the parking area near Har ki Pauri, and alighted out of it with the earthen pot containing the ashes of my father for immersion in the Ganga, a *Panda* accosted me and put the following personal questions. *"Kaun jat ho? Kahan se aaye ho? Gotra kya hai?* "(What is your caste? From where have you come? What is your *Gotra*?) He cross-checked the little information I provided to him with other *Pandas* present there. After mutual discussion, they told me that Keshav Pandit was my family priest.

With the *asthi* (ashes) urn dangling in my hand, and accompanied by my family, I sauntered slowly towards the *asthi* ghat at Har ki Pauri. There I met Keshav Pandit, who was already waiting for me. The Pandas of Hardwar have fast network of communal bonding and reciprocal cooperation. Keshav Pandit took charge of the immersion rites, chanted mantras from the *Vedas* and other scriptures, invoked certain gods, made me recall my ancestors, and helped me immerse the ashes of my father in accordance with the *Vedic* rituals. Every time he recited a mantra, he asked me for my *Gotra*, and I told him that my *Gotra* was Vats. It was for the first time that I came to know the importance of *Gotra*. And at the same time, I could discover my roots and identity that I am a descendant of Rishi Vats.

After the immersion ritual was over, I scampered to the office of Keshav Pandit for recording my visit, and the purpose of the visit, in his record book. He asked me as to when did someone from my family last visit Hardwar for the immersion of the ashes. I told him: "When my grandmother died." He further enquired: "When did she die?" "Perhaps in 1968," I replied. Keshav then asked his assistance: "Pandit Ji *1968 se aaj tak ki bahi lana*" (bring the record book from 1968 till date). The man addressed Panditji soon came out carrying six-inch thick, more than two-feet long, stack of papers bound in green cloth, typically folded once over. Each *bahi* (the record book) contained hundreds of pages. Keshav Pandit flipped the long pages of *bahi,* scanned through them. Lo and behold, he put before me the account recorded by my father in his own hand that he had come to Hardwar for the immersion of ashes of his mother.

This was clue enough for Keshav Pandit to unfold my family history. He turned the pages of *bahi* and told me that my grandfather had three sons, and one daughter, that the eldest son died in 1930, and the daughter a year later, that my mother died in 1948, and that my father had come with her ashes to immerse in the Ganga the same year, and so on and so forth. He even traced from his mighty *bahi* my family tree up to 1905, when my grandfather and maternal grandfather came together for the immersion of the ashes of their kith and kin. My grandfather recorded his visit in *bahi,* as also the full details of the family then existing, in Urdu. Since I know Urdu, I read what my grandfather had recorded in his own hand. This made me highly emotional and tears wallowed out of my eyes. It was a captivating, nay an emotive experience, for me. I felt as if I was having a face-to-face meeting with my ancestors. I now know my roots down to my grandfather, almost down to six generations. And I also know my identity that I am a descendant of sage Vats.

Almost every Hindu family has its hereditary *purohit* at Hardwar. The *Pandas* (family purohits) are an important institution, a constituent, of Hardwar. They perform the religious rites of the pilgrims, and record their visits. Their record books contain records of pilgrims, their names, castes, the places they hail from, the names of their fathers, grandfathers, brothers, sisters, the religious functions they came for and their signatures. I too recorded my visit in Keshav's *bahi* together with the information of my family, son, daughter, brother and sisters, for the future generation to know its roots. Those who want to discover their past, their roots, their identity, their quest will end with the family *purohit* at Hardwar. My tryst with the Spiritual India, which began at Badrinath, accentuated at the temple of bells, was complete at Hardwar.

The legends and myths related to the spiritual India of the *Rishis* and sages, who invented and laid down the rules for conventions, rituals and rites, are not only absorbing and stimulating, but they have relevance for all times. In fact, India is a rich store-house of stories, tales, legends and myths. *Panchtantra, Kathasaritasagara, Baital Pachisi, Hitopadesa*, are some of the examples, which are very popular both with the children as well as with the grown-ups. And the stories, legends appertaining the lives and actions of the sages of ancient India, not only vivify our hoary past, but they also tell us "who are we, and what and whence are we?"

We must not condemn our forefathers and ancestors

for having been what they were, or ourselves for being somewhat different from them. Our task is to relate ourselves to their environment, to bridge the distance of time and space, and separate the transitory from the permanent.

At the core of all historical religions, there are fundamental spiritual experiences, which the holy books express with various degrees of clarity. The seers of India illustrate and illuminate these primary experiences. Nothing is sacred to man than his own history. As memorials of the past, the sages are worth our attention. We cannot, and must not, judge our ancient seers and saints from the present standards. The philosophy of the sages of pre-*Vedic* and post-*Vedic* era, which seems to us today to be trivial, tedious, and almost unmeaning, should have had value and significance at the time when that was propounded. When we read the seers in order to know them, we cannot help being impressed by the exceptional ability, earnestness and ripeness of mind. For ripeness is all. The sages who tackled multifarious problems remain still, and will remain for all times to come, in essential harmony with the highest ideals of civilization. If we have to understand the socio-religious philosophy, and spiritual ideas of the seers, then we must know the atmosphere in which they worked. We must not judge the ancient sages from our standards. The irreligion of our time is largely the product of the supremacy of the materialism over the spiritualism, of the body over the soul. There are many dissatisfied souls who are "possessed" by the spirit of the west.

The question arises as to how could the sages and saints obtain wisdom and perfect purity of mind through penance. The answer is: "by the repression of their animal passions; by meditation; and by the mortification of the flesh, and the complete control over all the senses. "They strove to destroy the three strongest passions to which man is subject, namely *"zar, zun, and zameen* "(wealth, woman and land).

They freed themselves from all prejudices in respect of caste, rank and honour. In fact, they personified "high thinking and simple living."

The present standards of living and thinking are far different from that of the hoary past. Today the old binding culture is being broken. The ethical standards are dissolving. There is general ferment in the air, inward stirring and cultural crisis. It is time for us to go to our spiritual past, to immerse ourselves in spiritual tide. When that happens, we will see a ray of something novel on the horizon, something unprecedented. It will be the beginning of the spiritual renaissance.

In order to discover ourselves, our identity, we must turn to our traditional life, our scriptures, our classics, our sages and saints. Our seers have done more to colour our minds than we generally acknowledge. There is much in our past which is life-giving and elevating. Let us turn over together the treasures the wise men have left for us. The *Rishis* were *karam yogis*. They lived a full life, and discharged with the greatest diligence the manifold duties. "Life is for living and for living well," seems to have been their motto. They believed in the dictum: "renunciation not of life, but in life."

One may ask a pertinent question: "Where have all the *Rishis* gone? They are not seen these days." They are very much here. They are meditating in the crevices of the Himalayas, and in some hidden caves of Kedarnath, Badrinath, Gangotri and Yamnotri. These sages have chosen to move away, far from the madding crowd of civilization. Freeing themselves of the shackles of humdrum, mundane life, they have moved to the remote areas in order to attain ultimate peace and *moksha* (liberation).

**Dr. C. D. VERMA**

# 1.RISHI VASISHTA: THE RIVALS

# DRAMATIS PERSONAE

GUNADHYA: The narrator of the story

VASISHTA: A prominent seer of the *Vedic* era

VISWAMITRA: A famous sage, who was contemporary of *Rishi* Vasishta

SUDAS: The king of the Bharata principality during the *Vedic* age.

INDRA: The chief of the demigods

BRAHMA: The creator God

KALMASHA-PADA: A king who later became a demon because of a curse

SHAKTI: Son of sage Vasishta

ADRUSHYANTI: Saint Shakti's wife

NANDINI: The divine cow

RAJA HARISH CHANDRA: A king of the Raghu dynasty, and an ancestor of Lord Rama

A group of disciples of sage Vasishta in the seer's hermitage

A brahman

# RISHI VASISHTA: THE RIVALS

## PROLOGUE

The story of the birth of sage Vasishta is quite interesting. It is said that he was born of *Apsara* (the celestial woman) Urvasi from Mitra and Varuna. There appears a hymn in the *Rig Veda* which says: "Thou, O Vasishta, art the son of Mitra and Varuna, born a Brahmin from the soul of Urvasi." Varuna, in a way, was the father of Vasishta.

Who are Varuna and Mitra? Varuna is a divine being. He is one of the oldest of the *Vedic* deities, a personification of all-investing sky, king of the universe, and king of gods and men. He is in possession of illimitable knowledge. This divine being is believed to have fashioned both earth and heaven. He is often connected with Mitra; Varuna being the ruler of the night, and Mitra of the day. (Mitra is probably connected with the Persian "Mithra," a form of the sun). But in the *Vedas*, he is generally associated with Varuna, being the rulers of the day and night respectively.

In the aforementioned hymn of the *Rig Veda*, it is mentioned: "When the two Aditya (Adityas were the celebrated deities of whom Varuna was the chief. Consequently, he was the Aditya. Aditya is also the name of the sun), Mitra and Varuna beheld *Apsara* Urvasi at a sacrifice. Their seed fell from them. It fell on many places, into a jar, into the water, on the ground. *Muni* Vasishta was produced on the ground, while *Rishi* Agastya was born of the jar. "The reference to Vasishta's birth from the gods Mitra-

Varuna, is a clear pointer that he is invested with a kind of divinity.

## CURTAIN RAISER

My name is Gunadhya. I am actually a celestial being. I came to the earth in the world of mortals as a story-teller. I was the narrator of the tales in Somdeva's famous book *Kathasaritasagara (KATHA-SARITA-SAGARA)*, that is the Ocean of Stories. And I am going to perform the same role of a narrator in telling the story of sage Vasishta, and his rivalry with *Rishi* Viswamitra. I will tell as to how the rivalry between the two seers shaped the ancient history in the *Vedic* age. In fact, the clash between Vasishta and Viswamitra, the seers great, brought about a complete metamorphosis in the social, religious and political ambience in the *vedic* era.

Vasishta, who is traditionally regarded as the author of the seventh *Mandala* of the *Rig Veda*, is one of the most interesting personalities of the V*edic* age. Like *Rishi* Viswamitra, he has the distinction of being celebrated not only in the *Rig Veda*, but also in the later V*edic*, epic and classical literature. He is the subject of many mythologies. For example, he had Nandini, the daughter of Kamdhenu, the divine cow, who could grant him anything that he wanted. In the *Ramayana,* he is the family priest of the Raghu dynasty, and Guru of Lord Rama and his brothers. His ideas have been influential. He has been called as the first stage of the Vedanta school of philosophy by Adi Shankara.

He was both a political person as well as a seer. And

as a religious leader, he is distinguished for his remarkable spirit of tolerance and compromise. As a matter of fact, he is perhaps the only seer to whom some kind of divinity is attributed in the *Rig Veda*.

## ACT: ONE

## SCENE: 1

Gunadhya: What were those circumstances which engendered the clash between Vasishta and Viswamitra, and which eventually accentuated into the rivalry between the two sages. There was a king named Sudas who frequently appears in the *Rig Veda*. In his court the rival sages, Vasishta and Viswamitra, are represented as living. Sudas was the king of the Bharata, a principality of war-like people. Bharatas are frequently mentioned in the *Rig Veda*. The name is sometime mixed up with that of Viswamitra. Bharatas' sons were called Viswamitras, and Viswamitra's sons were called Bharatas. The reason for this mix-up was that Viswamitra was the *purohit* (priest) of Sudas. Bharatas were making rapid progress under the military leadership of Sudas and priestly guidance of Viswamitra.

There was another principality named Tritsus. The people of Tritsus are also regularly mentioned in the *Rig Veda*. Sudas wanted Tritsus and Bharata principalities to come together. Rishi Vasishta was the most powerful person among the Tritsus, as he was their priest. In order to forge an alliance between the two peoples (of Bharatas and Tritsus), king Sudas approached Vasishta.

Sudas: *Rishi* Vasishta! I am the king of the Bharata. My people are making steady progress in every field.

But the Tritsus tribe is inimical to us. Since you are their priest and highly influential person, I want you to help bring both the principalities -Bharata and Tritsus-together. And I know that you can perform this errand successfully.

Vasishta: And what would I gain out of this alliance?

Sudas: I will make you the official priest of Bharatas.

Vasishta: It is true that I aspire to be the priest of Bharatas. But that would hurt *Rishi* Viswamitra, who is presently officiating as the priest of the Bharatas. If I replace him, he will feel humiliated and annoyed.

Sudas: Don't worry about Viswamitra's annoyance. I know how to deal with him. I want Bharata and Tritsus to come closer, as it will bring peace, harmony and prosperity for both the peoples.

Gunadhya: Vasishta succeeded in the negotiations, and brought about political and military alliance between Bharata and Tritsus. Sudas felt obliged. He dismissed his original *Purohit* Viswamitra, and appointed Vasishta in his place. As a result of that alliance, the Bharatas and Tritsus came to form a single political and military unit. Thus, the seeds of the feud between the families of Vasishta and Viswamitra, are perhaps to be found in this ancient historical event.

## SCENE: 2

Gunadhya: Thus, plagued and beleaguered by the ignominy suffered at the hands of king Sudas, who removed him as the official priest of Bharatas, Viswamitra decided to take revenge.

Viswamitra: I must avenge my humiliation, and teach a lesson to Sudas, and his newly appointed *Purohit* Vasishta. I will now form a confederation of war-lords to take on Sudas.

Gunadhya: Rishi Viswamitra, then, formed a confederation of older kings, and prepared an aggressive plan to resist Sudas and Vasishta. He succeeded in forming a military alliance of ten prominent war –lords who represented the *Vedic* Indians as well the non-Aryan Indians. Then ensued a battle between Bharatas and Tritsus on one side and the confederation of the war-lords on the other, traditionally known as *Dasa-rajna Yuddha* (war of ten kings).

Sudas ultimately won the war, and the Bharatas attained political dominance. This early political supremacy of the Bharatas, seems to have given India her name as "Bharatvarsh. "It is claimed that it was not only the military might of Sudas that was responsible for the victory, but the cooperation and blessings of Vasishta also. For more efficacious, perhaps in this connection, was the magical / spiritual potency of the mantras of Rishi Vasishta. The reference to *Dasa-rajna Yuddha*, appears in the *Rig Veda* in Vasisht *mandala suktas*.

## SCENE: 3

Gunadhya: The relation between Vasishta and Viswamitra forms an important chapter in the social history of the *vedic* as well as of the post-*vedic* period. The feud between the two sages, both powerful enough, continued for long. It got aggravated when Viswamitra wanted to take Nandini, a divine cow, by force. The cow was a gift to Vasishta by Lord Indra.

Vasishta: Lord Indra! I have my hermitage on the banks of the river Saraswati. My daily routine is to teach my disciples, and to practice austerities. A large number of visitors come to the hermitage to meet me. In order to feed and entertain all of them, I need a large quantity of milk and curd and also ghee for the performance of *yagnas* (sacrifices) regularly. Therefore, I want you to help me overcome the insufficiency of milk and ghee.

Lord Indra: All the *devtas* (demigods) are pleased with your *tapasya* (penance) and sacrifices. I, therefore, gift you a divine cow. It is Nandini, daughter of Kamdhenu. As the divine cow, it has special qualities. Nandini will give you plenty of milk which will meet all the requirements of the hermitage.

Besides, it will fulfill all the material needs. Since it has moon-like patches all over its body, it is also called "Shabala", which literally means multi-coloured.

Gunadhya: Viswamitra, before he became a sage, was originally a king. Once it so happened that king Viswamitra went for hunting. While wandering in the forest in search of game, he and his men, got tired. Perchance, they saw the hermitage of sage Vasishta. Since the king and his men were hungry and thirsty, they felt that they would get food and water in the hermitage. So, they entered the hermitage.

Vasishta: I welcome you king! Since you and your army are my guests, please take some rest here. In the meantime, I will make arrangements to serve you with refreshments to satiate your hunger and slake your thirst.

Gunadhya: The sage Vasishta fed the king and his retinue with all kinds of dainties and delectable dishes. This surprised the king. He wondered as to how a sage, living in the forest, could arrange such sumptuous food for such a large number of people.

Viswamitra: O sage! How is it that living isolated in the forest with no visible means of support, you were able to provide such a lavish feast for me and my men? Is it the result of some great magic? Or is it owing to the celestial blessings that you have been provided with the means to entertain your guests thus.

Vasishta: O King! What you saw was no magic. Lord Indra has gifted me Nandini, the divine cow. Like her mother, Kamdhenu, this sacred cow represents plenty, gives me all that I want, milk, curd, ghee. Thanks to her that I was able to provide you with refreshments.

Gunadhya: The king felt that this divine cow could solve the problem of feeding his great army. So, he thought of taking the cow to his kingdom.

Viswamitra: O, great one! I shall give you ten thousand heads of first-class cattle. Give me Nandini in exchange. She will be very useful to me.

Vasishta: Listen King! It is not appropriate for me

to part with the gift given to me by Indra. It will annoy the demigods.

Viswamitra: (*Entering into arguments*) I will not violate any ethical norm. I shall take care of all the requirements of your hermitage. Give me Nandini.

Vasishta: Why should you bear the burden of this huge expenditure? If you have enough and plenty, then help your subjects with food-grains and other necessities of life. I do not wish to accept money from a king for the use of our *Ashram* (hermitage).

Gunadhya: The exchange of arguments continued. The refusal of Vasishta to part with Nandini angered the king. He asserted that whatever good things existed in his kingdom, they belonged to him. How could a poor sage like Vasishta say no to him, and be disrespectful to a king?

Viswamitra: Vasishta, listen! If you do not give the divine cow I desire, by your sweet will, then I will take her by force. I am a king. My writ will run.

Gunadhya: Viswamitra was highly arrogant; the kingship had clouded his mind. He decided to use force to take the cow away.

Viswamitra: Soldiers! Tie up this cow with ropes, and take her by force to our kingdom. I will see who stops me.

Gunadhya: The soldiers surrounded the cow, but the cow dodged them and darted away. Nandini came running to sage Vasishta.

Nandini: Sage! The king's soldiers are trying to

drag me by force. Master! tell me what wrong have I committed that you have so abandoned me.

Vasishta: Shabala! You have done no wrong. I have not abandoned you. Viswamitra is taking you by force. Since he is the king, and has the army at his disposal, he can arm-twist and use coercion, because for him might is right. Besides, he is my guest. How can I cause any harm to him!

Nandini: In that eventually, great saint, grant me the permission to subdue and vanquish the army of the king.

Gunadhya: Sage Vasishta nodded his head in agreement. Nandini bellowed aloud. By the divine power of her voice, thousands of magical soldiers came into being. They fought a pitch battle with the men of king Viswamitra, and trounced them. Viswamitra was defeated lock, stock, and barrel.

## SCENE: 4

Gunadhya: Viswamitra felt humiliated because of the defeat, despite the fact that he had a large army in tow. He burnt with desire to retaliate. He decided to undertake arduous *tapasya* (penance) to acquire powerful weapons. He sauntered to the forest post-haste. There he engaged himself in severe austerities. Eventually, he succeeded in acquiring the knowledge of archery and other divine weapons.

Viswamitra was not only arrogant but insolent also. Following the acquisition of divine weapons, he was swollen with pride. Consequently, he decided to defeat and destroy sage Vasishta. With this determination he came to the seer's hermitage, and began to rain arrows after arrows on the *Ashram*. The disciples and other saints present in the hermitage ran hither and thither. The disciples ran to sage Vasishta to seek his help.

Disciples: Sire! Viswamitra has ruined our *Ashram* with arrows and other weapons.

Vasishta: Don't be frightened. Don't lose courage. I know how to deal with an arrogant and insolent person. This staff in my hand will be sufficient to beat him and make him flee. (It is customary for the sages to carry a *danda*, that is staff, in their hands always).

Gunadhya: *Rishi* Vasishta came out of his hermitage, holding staff (Brahm danda) in his hands, and confronted and challenged Viswamitra.

Vasishta: O, you fool! Why are you destroying the hermitage? Have you cast aside all ethical and moral principles? It is the duty of a king to build and protect and not to destroy. I will punish you for your dereliction.

Viswamitra: I am shooting my arrows. Instead of making empty noise, defend your *Ashram*, if you can.

Vasishta: (*putting up his Brahm danda before him, the sage challenged the king*). Show me your valour and strength, you fool!

Gunadhya: Arrows, *agneyastra* even the *brahmastra*, hit the danda, and got reduced like burnt out coal and fell at the feet of the sage Vasishta. The power and strength of Vasishta's *tapasya* was concentrated in the staff of the seer. All the weapons shot by Viswamitra were rendered powerless before the powerful *danda* of *Rishi* Vasishta. In fact, the weapons fell at the feet of the sage.

Disciples: Sire! You are a great seer. Your strength, both temporal and spiritual, is beyond our ken. Honorable sir! Now calm down and control yourself.

Gunadhya: Viswamitra was defeated. He realised his mistake. He understood the truth.

Viswamitra: I took the wrong path. It is impossible to suppress the truth by force. There is no value for my temporal power and strength. The real power comes from *tapasya* (penance). All my divine weapons have been rendered ineffective owing to the power of penance of Vasishta. If I have to vanquish him, I must become equal to him. And that can be possible only through penance.

Gunadhya: Viswamitra abdicated his throne. He handed over the reins of his kingdom to his son, and left for the Himalayas for severe penance. He engrossed himself in stern austerities, and eventually became a famous *Rishi* (seer).

## SCENE: 5

Gunadhya: There was a king named Kalmasha-pada. He was a king of the solar dynasty (*Suryavanshi*), and a son of Sudas. He was the ancestor of Lord Rama. He was famed for his learning. Originally, his name was Pravriddha. His feet had become disfigured when they came in contact with water that had been charmed with incantations for a curse. Hence his name Kalmasha-pada, that is "blemished – feet. "

According to a legend told in the *Mahabharata,* king Kalmasha-pada, while hunting in the forest, came across Shakti, the eldest son of *Rishi* Vasishta. The king asked Shakti to move aside and give him the way. But Shakti refused to give way to the chariot of the king. During those days, the tradition and the practice was that if a chariot of a king came in the way of a saint, a cow, a blind man, an old man, a man carrying a load, or a pregnant woman, the king's vehicle and entourage, would give the right of way to them by moving aside. That was considered the appropriate conduct. But in the instant case things turned out to be different.

Kalmasha-pada:  Please move to a side, and give way to the chariot. Don't you know that I am a king?

Shakti: Don't you know that I am a sage? It is enjoined upon the king to make way for a saint. Your thinking is erroneous to accost a seer thus.

Kalmasha-pada: (*Asserting with a king's highly arrogant look*). Let me show you the power of a king.

Gunadhya: The king became angry. He took out the horse-whip and hit Shakti hard. The action of the king irritated the saint, and peeved at his audacity, he cursed him.

Shakti: You scoundrel! You whip a saint. Your temperament is that of *Rakshasa.* Therefore, I curse you to become a *Rakshasa* (demon).

Gunadhya: When this exchange of words was going

on, Viswamitra happened to pass that way. He overheard the conversation. He was angry with the king. He wanted Kalmasha-pada to become his disciple, but the king refused. And his enmity with Vasishta impelled him to make use of this opportunity and punish both king Kalmasha-pada and Shakti, the son of Vasishta. By his yogic powers, he caused a demon named Kinkra enter the body of the king. After this incident, the king decided to return home. On his way back, he met a Brahman.

Brahman: King! I am hungry. Please give me some food.

Gunadhya: The king reached his palace. He asked the cook to prepare a meal of human flesh mixed with rice and feed it to the Bahman. When the food was offered to the Brahman, he saw through his spiritual sight that food was unholy. He reacted:

Brahman: King Kalmasha-pada! Since you have served me unholy food made from human flesh, I curse you that hence onward you will develop appetite for human flesh. You will be turned into a human-eating demon.

Gunadhya: The curse, thus reinforced, became strong. He again went to the forest to the hermitage of Shakti, and called him out:

Kamasha-pada: Shakti! Owing to your curse, my sense of righteousness has been destroyed. I am reduced to a dreaded state of a cannibal. Since you are responsible for what I have become, I will take revenge and eat you up.

Gunadhya: Kalmasha-pada, the king turned

*Rakshasa,* ate Shakti. Subsequently he ate the brothers of Shakti also. The death of his sons caused unbearable grief to *Rishi* Vasishta. He went away from home and wandered in the forest aimlessly. Suddenly, he espied Adrushyanti, the widow of Shakti. She was pregnant. She had come to the forest in search of her father-in-law, sage Vasishta. The sage was moved to pity when he saw her. He brought her to the hermitage. He caressed her with love and affection. After a few days she gave birth to a son, who was named Parashara.

One day Vasishta, accompanied by Adrushyanti, went to the forest to collect twigs for the sacrifice in the a*shram.* Suddenly Adrushyanti, saw a *Rakshasa* (demon) who moved towards her threateningly as if to kill and eat her. She ran towards Vasishta and sought his protection. The seer asked her to relax. The sage looked towards the demon, made a big sound, and the *Rakshasa* stood still fixed at the spot, unable to move even a step.  Using his divine vision, the seer saw that it was the king Kalmasha-pada. He could also envision about what had happened. Taking some water out of his water jug, he sprinkled it on him. The king-turned demon, was freed from his curse.

Kalmasha-pada: O, great sage! Because of the curse, I became a demon, and did what I should not have done. You are kind enough to free me from the curse. I fall upon your feet, and beg of you to forgive me.

Vasishta: (*Kalmasha-pada had wronged the seer immensely. He had committed grave crime. But the sage was known for his tolerance and forgiveness*). O, king! Go back to your kingdom, and rule over your people in a just and fair manner, the way you did before. Do not go against righteousness. Treat preceptors and elders with respect. Shed arrogance. Power and wealth had made you vain. Because of these characteristic and temperamental faults, you were punished in the past.

Gunadhya: Kalmasha-pada returned home. He was saved and reformed by a great and noble soul, that is sage Vasishta. Prashara, the son of Shakti, wanted to take revenge from the king Kalmasha –pada for killing his father. But *Rishi* Vasishta dissuaded him:

Vasishta: Son! you have mastered all the four *Vedas*, and earned a great power through your penance. Therefore, it does not behove you to kill Kalmasha-pada. Parashra! You are a great saint. You should have tolerance and patience. There is no virtue greater than patience. Kalmasha-pada is the king of our country. He is ruling righteously. It will be a sin to kill him. If you kill him, your father is not likely to come back. Rather, the kingdom will become rudderless. The denizens will be put to a lot of hardship. Your father also committed a grave error. He should not have quarreled with the king. He should have shown tolerance and patience and given way to the king and his entourage. In a way, he became a cause of his own death.

## SCENE: 6

Gunadhya: Harish Chandra was the king of Ayodhya. He always spoke the truth, and nothing except the truth. In the local parlance, he was called "Satyawadi "(truthful). Once Lord Indra held his court in the heaven. He posed a question to those who were present in his court, including Vasishta and Viswamitra.

Indra: Who is truthful on the earth?

Vasishta: Raja Harish Chandra is the most truthful. How-so-ever trying the circumstances may be, he will never utter a lie.

Viswamitra: (*Since Viswamitra harboured ill-will against Vasishta, he stood up, and intervened*): "Devraj Indra! what Vasishsta says is not true. Since he is the preceptor of the King of Ayodhya, he has said what he has said, out of partiality for his disciple. He is biased. We should not believe him. Is there a man on the earth who will not speak a lie when confronted with hard and difficult situation?

Vasishta: I do not agree with Viswamitra. Harish Chandra will never utter a lie, whatever may be hardship, trials and tribulations.

Viswamitra: Look! I shall compel Harish Chandra to speak lies. If I fail in my endeavour, I will pass on all the merit of my *tapasya* to him.

Gunadhya: Vasishta returned to his hermitage. He knew that Harish Chandra would be subjected to severe tests and trials. But he was sure that Harish Chandra will not tell a lie, and will always remain steadfast to speak the truth. Viswamitra used all the stratagems to test Harish Chandra. His hatred for Vasishta was the only reason for his entering into the controversy. He manipulated through duplicity and cunning to prove his point. He took from Harish Chandra his kingdom; he was made a debtor; his queen Chandramati and his son Rohitaswa had to leave him and go to Kashi. Even there he was pestered to pay the loan. He sold himself and his wife to pay back the loan. He was forced to serve as a watchman in a cemetry in Kashi. His son died because of the snake bite. But nothing could compel Harish Chandra to tell a lie. Viswamitra failed in his repeated attempts to coerce Harish Chandra to utter a lie. He eventually accepted his defeat, and made over the merit of his *tapasya* (penance) to Harish Chandra. Vasishta was proven right.

Viswamitra then went to the forest for yet another round of *tapasya* (penance).

## SCENE: 7

Gunadhya: Notwithstanding the repeated attempts made by Viswamitra to vanquish Vasishta, he could not succeed. This increased his frustration and anger manifold. He wanted to become equal to Vasishta in merit and power. So, he decided to undertake severe *tapasya* to achieve his aim. And it was necessary also since he had passed on the merit of his penance to Raja Harish Chandra as aforementioned.

At last, Viswamitra went to the forest once again. There he did harsh penance for many years. At long last Lord Brahma manifested himself to him and asked:

Brahma: Viswamitra! I am pleased with your penance. Please ask for the boon.

Viswamitra: I want to become equal in merit to Vasishta. Therefore, Sire, grant me the wish that I should be acknowledged as "Brahamarshi "(a top status for a self-realized sage) like Vasishta.

Gunadhya: Lord Brahma ruminated over the wish and felt that Viswamitra, despite having done stern penance, failed to free his mind of *"Aham "*(arrogance). He told Viswamitra:

Brahma: Viswamitra! You are a great sage. But you have not yet reached the stage of Vasishta and earned his merit. He will not accept you as "Brahamarshi." (*Having said that Brahma disappeared*).

Gunadhya: Viswamitra was further irked and disappointed by the curt reply of Lord Brahma. He felt that he gave up the kingdom, came to the forest, did severe penance, and yet he has not earned the credentials to be acknowledge as "Brahamarshi." He resolved to meet Vasishta to find out the reasons from him for not agreeing to his becoming the "Brahamarshi." So, he came to the hermitage of Vasishta, and perforce entered the hut. Vasishta was sitting with his wife Arundhati. The moment Arundhati saw Viswamitra, she was frightened. But Vasishta remained calm and quiet.

Vasishta: Look Arundhati! How arrogant and vain Viswamitra is! What is the use of doing *tapasya*, if he cannot imbibe virtues like peace and calmness of mind? It is his *"Aham"* ("I", arrogance) that impedes his way to become a "Brahamarshi."

Gunadhya: Having heard the reprimand of Vasishta, Viswamitra realised his mistake. He felt that it was his ego that killed his merit. At last, the wisdom dawned on him. He belatedly understood the simple fact that he could not shed his ego, despite *tapasya*. He felt ashamed of his conduct. He repented of his behaviour.

Viswamitra: (*He prostrated before Vasishta, and pleaded)* "I realize my fault. Kindly forgive me.

Vasishta: Viswamitra! You have performed austere *tapasya*. But the aim of your *tapasya* was to gain fame, to gain power, to perform miracles. A saint must abandon the feelings of selfishness, arrogance and vanity. God only dwells in the clean and pure mind, and not in the mind of a person clinging to ego.

Viswamitra: *(prostrating before Vasishta, Viswamitra supplicated)*: Sire! You are my preceptor. Forgive me and bless me.

Vasishta: Be it so. I bless you from my heart.

# Epilogue

The rivalry between the two distinguished Vedic seers has virtually influenced even the later literary and social history of India. The feud between the two has been elaborated in the post –*Vedic* scriptures and literature. One thing, however, is quite certain that the seeds of this clash are traceable, to some extent, in the *Rig Veda* itself.

Nevertheless, the rivalry between Vasishta and Viswamitra eventually had a salubrious ending. Viswamitra left the hermitage. His ego was mortified. His rivalry and enmity with Vasishta died instantly. He was rid of rancor. His mind became purified. He performed more *tapasya*, more severe and austere than before. Lord Brahma was pleased. He granted the wish of Viswamitra, and pronounced: "You are a Brahamarshi now!"

From that day onwards both the sages, Vasishta and Viswamitra, became great friends. The credit for bringing about the change in the life and conduct of Viswamitra, goes to Vasishta. What a noble soul *Rishi* Vasishta was!

*****

# 2. RISHI VISWAMITRA: "TRISANKU" AND THE SECOND HEAVEN

## DRAMATIS PERSONAE

GUNADHYA: The narrator of the story

GADHI: King, father of Viswamitra

SATYAVATI: Daughter of king Gadhi

RICHIKA: A sage

VISWAMITRA: A renowned *Vedic* seer

VASISHTA: A sage, contemporary of *Rishi* Viswamitra

VARUNA: A vedic deity

HARISH CHANDRA: King of Ikshwaku dynasty

ROHIT: Son of king Harish Chandra

SATYAVRATA: A king of Ikshwaku dynasty, an ancestor of Lord Rama

TRISANKU: King Satayvrata who later came to be called Trisanku

MENAKA: An *apsara* (celestial nymph) who broke the *tapasya* of Viswamitra

INDRA: Chief of demigods

SUNAH-SHEPA: Adopted son of Viswamitra

AJIGARTA: Father of Sunha-shepa

SHAKTI: Son of *Rishi* Vasishta

Mother of Satyavati

# RISHI VISWAMITRA: "TRISANKU" AND THE SECOND HEAVEN

## PROLOGUE

Viswamitra's rivalry, to the point of enmity, and the consequential turn of events, leading to the battle of ten kings, called *Dasa-rajna Yuddha*, seems to have far reaching effects on the future course of India's cultural history. There is no gainsaying the fact that sage Viswamitra was the man of great consequence.

Viswamitra was originally born as *kshatriya*. But later on, through austerities, he raised himself to the rank of a Brahman. He gradually increased the rigor of his mortification till he successfully earned the titles of *Rajrishi, Devarshi, and Brahamarshi. Brahamarshi* is born of the mind of Brahma. *Devarshi* is the saint of lower rank. And a *Rajrishi* is virtually a king, who becomes a *Rishi* through knowledge and austerities, such as Raja Janaka. Viswamitra has the distinction of achieving all the three ranks of *Rishis*.

The events leading to his birth make an interesting story. According to the *Balmiki Ramayana (Bal Kand)*, there was a king named Kusha (not to be confused with Kusha, son of Lord Rama), a brain-child of Brahma. And Kusha's son was Kushanabha, a powerful and righteous prince. He was renowned by the name of Gadhi. He was the king of Kanya-kubja. Viswamitra was Gadhi's son. He succeeded his father and ruled for many years.

## CURTAIN RAISER

My name is Gunadhya. I am actually a celestial

being. I came to the earth in the world of mortals as a story-teller. I was the narrator of the tales in Somdeva's famous book *Kathasaritasagara (KATHA-SARITA – SAGARA)*, that is the Ocean of Stories. And I am going to perform the same role of a narrator in telling the story of *Rishi* Viswamitra, and his creation of the Second Heaven for Trisanku, who was originally a king, named Satyavrata.

Viswamitra is one of the most venerated sages of the ancient India. He is traditionally regarded as the author of the third *Mandala* of the *Rig Veda*. In fact, he is one of the most enigmatic and intriguing personalities of the *Vedic* age. His influence has extended far beyond the Vedic era. He is one of the few seers who is frequently celebrated in the later Vedic, and the classical literature. He has played a significant role in the socio-historial, religious and literary fields. And to cap it all, he is the reputed author of the holiest of the mantras in the *Rig Veda*, namely the *Gayatri Mantra*. Owing to the *Gayatri Mantra*, recited by every Hindu family in India and abroad, he has left a lasting impression on generations down the ages.

## ACT: ONE

## SCENE: 1

Gunadhya: The story of Viswamitra's birth and dynasty appears in the *Vishnu Purana*, as also in the *Mahabharata*. The history has it that Gadhi had a daughter named Satyavati (not to be confused with Satyavati of the *Mahabharata*). *Rishi* Richika, who was foremost among the race of Bhrigu, wanted to marry her. But Gadhi rejected the proposal and refused to marry off his daughter to him. Firstly, because he was an old Brahman, and secondly, he was hot- tempered. In order to ward him off, he hit upon a plan.

Gadhi: Sage! I may agree to marry my daughter to you, provided you give me one thousand horses in return for my daughter. Please ensure that the horses should be fleet / swift of foot, and white in colour with black ears.

Gunadhya: Richika approached Varuna and requested him for one thousand horses as desired by Gadhi. Varuna obliged the saint. Richika gave the horses to Gadhi, and thus fulfilled the marriage condition. Gadhi was left with no choice. He eventually married off his daughter to the old Brahman. Both Satyavati and Richika wanted a son. Sage Richika performed a *yagna* (ritual) and gave *charu* (sacrificial mess) to Satyavati.

Satyavati: Swami! Give some *charu* to my mother also, so that she might also have a son.

Richika:  I will prepare a second bowl of *charu* for your mother. But it will have different ingredients.

Gunadhya: Sage Richika gave two different bowls of Charu to his wife Satyavati.

Richika: Satyavati! This bowl of sacrificial offering is for you, and the second one is for your mother. (*And the Rishi went off to the forest to meditate*).

Mother: Satyavati! Usually, people want good sons for themselves. They are not keen about obtaining a good brother-in-law. I, therefore, suspect that your *charu* is better than that of mine. Let us exchange them. I am a queen and my son will rule the world. Therefore, he must be strong. Your son will be a

Brahman. He has not to rule the world. He has not to be powerful.

Gunadhya: The mother and the daughter exchanged the bowls of *charu*. When Richika came back from forest and heard about what had happened, he was very angry.

Richika: You fool! What have you done? You disobeyed me to your detriment. In your mother's charu, I had put the ingredients for a son who would be brave and violent as a *kshatriya*. And into your bowl, I had put ingredients for a son who would be a non-violent and peaceful Brahman. You have turned everything topsy-turvy.

Satyavati: I beg your pardon for the mistake I committed. I did not know the consequences. I now request you to bless me with a grand-son who should be brave and violent.

Richika: Be it so!

Gunadhya: After a few months, the mother of Satyavati gave birth to a son who eventually came to be called and known as Viswamitra. And Satyavati gave birth to Jamad-agni, who married Renuka. Their son was Parashurama, who killed many *kshatriyas*.

## SCENE: 2

Gunadhya: Harish Chandra, a king of Ikshwaku race, and an ancestor of Rama, was childless. He approached *Devarishi* Narad who advised him to worship Varuna (a *Vedic* deity). Accordingly, the king propitiated god Varuna.

Varuna: King! I am pleased with your worship. Tell me your wish; what do you want?

Harish Chandra: Sire! I am childless. I want you to bless me with a son.

Varuna: Be it so. However. Your wish is granted on the stipulation that you would sacrifice your son to me.

Gunadhya: The king agreed to the stipulation. He was blessed with a son whom he named Rohit. But the king postponed, on one pretext or the other, to fulfill his vow. At last, Varuna reminded the king of his promise. When at length he resolved to perform the sacrifice, Rohit protested and left his house and went into the forest.

Varuna: King! You have failed to keep your promise. I, therefore, curse you to suffer from dropsy.

Gunadhya: When Rohit came to know of the dreaded disease afflicting his father, he thought of returning home. But he was dissuaded from going back and importuned to wander in the forest. While so wandering in the forest, he came across a Brahman, named Ajigarta who had three sons.

Rohit: Reverend Sir! You have three sons. I request you to part with one of your sons. In lieu of that I will give you one hundred cows plus gold as compensation.

Gunadhya: The Brahman agreed. Rohit purchased from Ajigarta his middle son, Sunah –shepa to be the substitute for himself in the sacrifice. He returned to his father and asked him to sacrifice Sunah-shepa to

Varuna in his place. Varuna agreed to this arrangement. Sunah-shepa was bound at the stake to be immolated. But he did not want to die. In fact, nobody wants to die. The sacrifice commenced. Many sages, including Viswamitra, Vasishta, Jamad-agni, were present. Sunah-shepa had heard about the yogic powers of Vaswamitra.

Sunah-shepa: Sage Viswamitra! Why I am being immolated in the sacrificial fire? I am still very young, and I want to live. Kind-hearted as you are, please save me with your spiritual powers.

Viswamitra:   I tell you two mantras; one to propitiate Lord Vishnu, and the other to please Indra. Please recite them. You will be rid of the trouble.

Gunadhya: Sunah-shepa recited the mantras as told by Viswamitra. His bonds became loose, and he eventually became free. King Harish Chandra was also cured of the disease. Varuna agreed to set him free. The priests, then, honoured Sunah-shepa by inviting him to participate in the sacrifice as a priest. Sunah-shepa agreed and completed the sacrifice in the proper manner.

Viswamitra: Sunah-shepa! I am extremely happy that your life has been saved. It is the marvel of the mantras that you recited. Since you have got second life due to the mantras that I taught you, I adopt you as my eldest son.

Ajigarta: Since he has escaped death, I supplicate to you, great sage, to give my son back to me.

Viswamitra: Lord Vishnu and Indra, whom he propitiated through mantras, have given Sunah-shepa to me; he will be my adopted son, and be known as

Devarata (given by the gods).

Sunah-shepa: Father! It is now impossible for me to return to the old family. *Rishi* Viswamitra's family is my new family.

Viswamitra: I designate Sunah-shepa the eldest of all my sons, and endow him with my divine inheritance.

Gunadhya: Viswamitra then told his sons toagree to acknowledge Sunah-shepa as their eldest brother. Half of the sons of Viswamitra greed, and the other half refused. Viswamitra, then, cursed those who refused to acknowledge Sunah-shepa as their eldest brother that their progeny would be living as outcasts. And those who acknowledged Devarata's seniority, were blessed to be prosperous in every way.

## SCENE: 3

Gunadhya: Viswamitra was not a Brahman by birth. He was a *Kshatriya*. Nevertheless, he had a serious characteristic infirmity. He was very quick to anger, which made him clash with Rishi Vasishta many a time. He even picked up quarrels with many other kings, sages and gods. However, his rivalry with Vasishta had brought about a complete metamorphosis in his life and idiosyncrasies.

Once he was returning with his army from an expedition. On the way he happened to pass close to the hermitage of Vasishta. The a*shram* was situated in a lush-green valley-glade with birds chirping and animals tip-toeing and wandering all around. Attracted by the salubrious surroundings, king Kaushika (Viswamitra) thought of entering the hermitage and rest for a while.

Vasishta: King! I welcome you to my *ashram*. Since you and your men are tired, please rest for some time here. In the meantime, I will arrange some refreshments for you.

Viswamitra: (*The sumptuous food offered by Vasishta highly satisfied as well surprised Viswamitra*). Rishi! Your hermitage is situated in isolation in the forest. I wonder as to how you could arrange such a huge quantity of refreshments to feed me and my army.

Vasishta: O king! This feast that you have partaken with your men, has been provided by Nandini, my divine cow. She is the daughter of Kamdhenu, Indra's divine Cow. She was gifted to me by Indra. She provides me with everything that I need.

Viswamitra: Sage! I need this cow more than you. She will provide food and sustenance to my large army. Please give Nandini to me.

Gunadhya: Rishi Vasishta politely refused. Viswamitra offered him huge wealth along with one thousand heads of cattle. But Vasishta could not be tempted. This annoyed Viswamitra. He ordered his army to seize the divine cow and take her to the kingdom. However, by yogic power, Vasishta, the great sage, brought forth an entire army of fierce warriors. They fought the army of Viswamitra, and defeated them.

The incident made a deep impression on king Kaushika (Viswamitra). He realized for the first time that the power obtained by *tapasya* (penance) was greater than the temporal power and the physical might. He renounced his kingdom and embarked on a quest to become greater sage than Vasishta.

## SCENE: 4

Gunadhya: There was yet another clash between the two sages. This clash is highly significant, because it brought about a complete transformation in the life and character of Viswamitra. Viswamitra, through *tapasya*, earned the knowledge of celestial weaponry. Filled with pride at this achievement, he came to Vasishta's hermitage, and caused great havoc; even killed the residents of the hermitage. *Rishi* Vasishta brought about his *braham-danda* (a wooden stick containing the power of Brahma himself). It consumed Viswamitra's most powerful weapons, and reduced them to ashes. Vasishsta even attempted to attack his tormentor, but the gods interjected in time and stopped him from doing the unthinkable. Viswamitra was defeated and humiliated once again at the hands of Vasishta.

Viswamitra fled from the scene. He again went to the forest for yet another round of *tapasya*. At last Lord Brahma appeared and bestowed on him the title of *Rajarshi* (the king who became a *Rishi*). In penance this time, he observed more severe and stern austerities.

## SCENE: 5

Gunadhya: Viswamitra was engrossed in harsh and intense penance. This frightened Indra, lest he should capture the heaven and supplant Indra and other gods. So, Indra decided to break his *tapasya* by hook or by crook.

Indra: Menaka! You are an *apsara* (celestial nymph). You were born from the churning of the ocean by *devas* (gods) and *asuras* (demons). You are one of the most beautiful, talented and intelligent *apsaras* in my court. *Rishi* Viswamitra is presently engaged in severe penance. If he succeeds in his *tapasya*, he will climb up the spiritual ladder, and might supplant me and other gods from the heaven. We are frightened. We suffer a sense of insecurity. Therefore, Viswamitra must be stopped in his tracks before he usurps the position as a king of *devas*. Please descend to the earth, lure Viswamitra and break his *tapasya* (penance).

Menaka: Lord Indra! I feel honoured for the task you have entrusted to me. I will do your bidding. I will assume the form of a charming damsel, bewitch and entice Viswamitra, and distract him from his penance.

Gunadhya: Menaka literally charmed *Rishi* Viswamitra. She aroused his passion, and thus broke his *tapasya*, and successfully completed her mission. The moment Viswamitra set his eyes on the celestial nymph, he was consumed with lust and passion. Eventually, Menaka genuinely fell in love with the sage. Instead of returning to the heaven, she resolved to spend some years in the company of the sage. After the romance and dalliance of some years, Menaka gave birth to a daughter.

Menaka: Seer dear! I have spent many years on the earth in your company. Now it is time for me to return to *Indrapuri*.

Viswamitra: I belatedly realize that I have been

tricked by Indra. Menaka! I love you deeply. I also know your feelings for me; you too love me. I, therefore, curse you to be separated from me forever. Since you are proud of your youth and beauty, I curse you that you would not possess this beauty in the next birth.

Gunadhya: Viswamitra left his daughter in the hermitage of sage Kanva, who named her Shakuntala. Many years later, Shakuntala fell in love with king Dushyanta, and gave birth to a son who was named Bharata. India, that is Bharat, is named after him.

## SCENE: 6

### *(STORY OF TRISANKU HEAVEN)*

Gunadhya: There was a king named Satyavrata. He was the son of King Prithu in the solar dynasty, and an ancestor of Lord Rama. As he grew old, he vacated the throne and made his son the King of Ayodhya in his place. Since he had lived a righteous life, Satyavrata's soul deserved ascension to the heaven, but he wished to do so with his mortal body. Satyavrata, in his effort to go to heaven with his physical body, became a Trisanku. King Satyavrata got the nomenclature of Trisanku, because he had committed three sins. First, while a prince, he misbehaved in the kingdom, and was temporarily exiled. Second, he killed a milch cow of sage Vasishta, his preceptor. And his third sin was that he used the unsanctified meat of his kill as food. The word Trisanku has another connotation. It denotes a middle ground between one's goals and desires, and one's current state.

The story of Trisanku is told by Balmiki in the *Bala*

*Kand* of his *Ramayana*. The story has it that when King Satyavrata became old, he handed over the reins of his kingdom to his son, Harish Chandra. Satyavrata was a highly religious person who followed the path of *dharma* and righteousness. He was a noble soul that deserved to ascend to the heaven. But he aspired to go to heaven with his corporeal body. In order to fulfill his desire, he approached his *guru* (preceptor) sage Vasishta.

Satyavrata: Sire! I have a desire to go to heaven with my body. Therefore, in order to fulfill my wish, please perform *yagna* (sacrifice, ritual) by which I can go to heaven while I am still alive.

Vasishta: Listen son! To send somebody to the heaven with earthly body, is not only unethical, but is also against the law of nature. Therefore, I will not perform the *yagna* to grant your unjust wish. Go and, do good deeds; they will take you to heaven when you die.

Gunadhya: Satyavrata could not be discouraged from his set goal, nor could he be dissuaded by the sound advice of his *guru*. He continued to make efforts to realize his desire. So, he approached *Rishi* Vasishta's son Shakti, who too was a great seer, to do what his father did not do.

Satyavrata: Shakti! You are the eldest son of *Guru* Vasishta. You are also a sage of great standing and reputation. I want to go to heaven with my body. Please perform the requisite *yagna* and send me to heaven. For performing this job, I will give you both pelf and power

Shakti: (*Seeing the audacity of Satyavrata, Shakti became angry*). Satyavrata! How dare you come to me with the demand, which my reverend father has already rejected. I will punish your insolence. I curse you to become a *chandal* (a person of low caste).

Gunadhya:   Owing to the curse, Satyavrata was transformed into a person smeared with ash, clothed in black, wearing iron jewelry. He was also afflicted by some disease. When he entered his kingdom looking thus, his subjects failed to recognize him and drove him out. Satyavrata, alias Trisanku, was forced to leave the country and wander in the wilderness. During his wanderings in the forest, he perchance met sage Viswamitra.

Satyavrata: Noble sage! I have a wish to go to the heaven with my mortal body. I had requested *Rishi* Vasishta to perform a *yagna* to send me to heaven while still alive. But he refused. Instead, he reprimanded me. I, then, went to his son, Shakti, with the same request, but instead of helping me out, he cursed me to become a *chandal*, in which condition I presently am.

Viswamitra:   I dislike Vasishta. I will teach him a lesson. What he did not do, I will do. First, I free you from the curse, and restore you to your original condition. I will perform the requisite ritual and send you to heaven with your earthly body.

Gunadhya: The *yagna* began. Viswamitra used his yogic power. And the king Trisanku started ascending to the heaven. The gods were alarmed by this unnatural happening. Trisanku had reached the gates of Heaven. Led by Indra, the demigods refused to permit Trisanku to enter, and tossed him down. Trisanku began falling back to the earth. The furious Viswamitra would not accept his defeat at the hands of Indra. The sage used his spiritual powers and arrested the fall of Trisanku, causing the latter to remain suspended mid-air upside-down.

Trisanku: Sage Viswamitra! I am stuck precariously between the sky and the earth, and remain suspended mid-air upside down. Please help me and undo the acts of *devas*.

Viswamitra: Who is Indra? He has the insolence of going against my will. King Trisanku! I will create another heaven, a parallel heaven, and another Indra.

Gunadhya: Viswamitra began the creation of a parallel heaven in the southern sky. When the new heaven was built, he put Trisanku in it. Then he began establishing Trisanku as the Indra of the new heaven. The demigods were frightened. They appeared before Rishi Viswamitra, consoled him, and appealed to him to refrain from this unnatural act.

Indra: Reverend sage! We are convinced of your powers. We have no quarrel with you. We only want to prevent an earthly mortal entering heaven with his corporeal body. Such an act is not only against the law of nature, but it puts the system of the earth into jeopardy.

Viswamitra: Indra! I agree with your arguments. But now Trisanku is confronted with a serious dilemma. If I bring him back to the earth, I will be breaking my own word. Let us reach a middle-path; let us strike a compromise. Let the king live in the new heaven that was created for him. The new heaven shall be called TRISANKU HEAVEN. The king shall live in this heaven from now onwards. He shall not supersede Indra's commands. And I assure the demigods that Trisanku will reside in the new heaven upside down.

Gunadhya: Trisanku remains suspended between the earth, to which he belonged, and the heaven that he sought. The phrase Trisanku is widely used in local parlance in India to describe a situation of "neither here nor there," to remain in limbo. Trisanku was succeeded by his son, Harish Chandra, a great king of solar dynasty, who is remembered for his truthfulness.

## EPILOGUE

The rivalry between the two distinguished *Vedic* seers, has actually influenced even later literary and social history of India. The feud between the two sages has been elaborated in the post-*Vedic* scriptures and literature. One thing, however, is quite certain that the seeds of this clash are traceable, to some extent, in the *Rig Veda* itself. Nevertheless, the rivalry between Vasishta and Viswamitra eventually had a salubrious ending. Viswamitra, through austerities, raised himself from the *Kshatriya* to the Brahman caste, and became a *Brahmarshi*, and attained an equality with his rival. Coincidently, both the *Rishis* were present during the *Ramayana* period. Vasishta was the kul-*guru,* that is the family priest, of Lord Rama. And Viswamitra too was the guru of Rama and Lakshmana, who decimated the demons troubling the *Rishis*. And it was Viswamitra who had brought both the brothers to the court of Raja Janaka, where Rama broke the *Shiv Dhanush*, and eventually married Sita. Further, the credit for bringing Rama to the dilapidated hermitage of sage Gautama also goes to Viswamitra. It was here that Rama, the incarnation of Vishnu, with the touch of his feet, freed Ahalya from the curse, and granted her the *moksha* (deliverance). This is a great spiritually fascinating and elevating event in the *Ramayana*.

Nevertheless, Viswamitra is a highly revered seer. His repute and standing rest on his creation of the GAYATRI MANTRA, which is also known as the SAVITRI MANTRA, for the Gayatri Mantra is dedicated to goddess Savitri, a deity of five elements. Gayatri is the name of the goddess of the *Vedic* Mantra.

The Gayatri Mantra is cited widely in the *Vedic* and post-*vedic* texts. The Gayatri Mantra is an important part of all rituals, religious discourses, and socio-religious ceremonies. It is recited day in and day out by the Hindus, not only in India, but all the world over. There have been varied translations and interpretations of the Gayatri Mantra:

**Om bhur bhuvah svah**
**Tat savitur varenyam**
**Bhargo devasaya dheemahi**
**Dhiyo yo nah prachodayat**

**Om**: *Param Brahm* (the Supreme Lord of the entire universe); **Bhur**: *Bhuloka* (physical plane)

**Bhuvah**: *Antriksha* (space); **Svah**: *Swarg-loka* (Heaven);

**Tat**: *Paramatma* (Supreme God). "Tat "literally means "that "Parmatama, because it defies description through speech or language, and that God is the ultimate Reality.

*Savitur:* Divine sun *(svara);* God is the ultimate Light of the wisdom, not to be Confused with the ordinary sun;

*Varenyam:* Fit to be worshipped, to be adored

**Bhargo:** Illumination. Remover of sins and ignorance; **Devasaya:** Divine grace, glory

(knowledge personified); **Dheemahi:** We contemplate, meditate; **Dhiyo:** *Buddhi*

(intellect); **Yo:** who; **Nah:** Requesting, urging, praying; **Prachodayat:** Enlighten.


'Om' is also written as 'AUM. '
A: emerges from the throat, originating in the region of the navel.
U: rolls over the tongue
M: ends on the lips

It is the sum and substance of the words that can emanate from the human throat. It is the primordial fundamental sound symbolic of the universal Absolute. Various scholars and saints have interpreted the Gayatri Mantra differently. For example-

Swami Vivekananda: "We meditate on the glory of that being who has produced that universe; may He enlighten our minds. "

Sri Aurobindo: "We adore the Supreme light of the divine sun; we inspire that it may impel our minds." He further elaborates: "The sun is the symbol of divine Light that is coming down, and Gayatri gives expression to the aspiration asking that divine Light to come down and give impulsion to all activities of the mind."

Dr S. Radhakrishnan: "We meditate on the adorable glory of the radiant Sun; may he inspire our intellect."

There is no gainsaying the fact that the Gayatri Mantra recommends belief in the purifying divine insight, and inspires understanding of intellect, and makes us choose the right path. It suggests "bhoor "which implies existence, and signifies "prana" (life, or the life breath). It also connotes "tat" meaning "that" -offer of praise to Him. The word "tat" also indicates a selfless belief and practice. "Savitur" indicates God's existence as a fountain from which spring forth all life and all things; which emanate from God and return to Him. "Bhargo" is the purifying of the intellect. We are purified and cleansed by His grace; God destroys our sins and afflictions. And we at last reach a state of unity and oneness with the Supreme Lord. When we become one with Him, we are rid of all impurities.

And there lies the magnitude of the Gayatri Mantra, and its relevance to the human life. Verily, the credit for creating such a magnificent life-inspiring, and life-purifying Mantra, goes to *Rishi* Viswamitra. Even if he had not done anything else in his life, Gayatri Mantra alone would have made him immortal.

So much so, even Lord Krishna refers to the Gayatri-prayer in the *Gita* (Chapter 10: verse 35):

*Vrihatsama tatha samnam*
*Gayatri chhandsam-aham*

(I am the Sam Veda among scriptures and the Gayatri among verses). It is important to realize that recitation of the Gayatri Mantra brings automatic salvation. Gayatri is a prayer. The worshipper is not able to resolve his doubts by his own intelligence; he does not know what is right and what is wrong. So, Krishna is the Gayatri by which the hapless devotee surrenders himself to Him. The Gayatri-prayer is doubtlessly propitious, for by this the worshipper seeks refuge in Krishna.

*****

# 3.RISHI MATANG AND SAINT SHABRI

## DRAMATIS PERSONAE

GUNADHYA: The narrator of the story

MATANG: A renowned seer and *Guru* of Shabri

LORD RAMA: incarnation of god Vishnu

LAKSHMANA: Younger brother of Lord Rama

SHABRI: A low-caste woman – saint, a devotee of Lord Rama

BHILRAJ:  Father of Shabri

MOTHER-ASS: An animal that tells Matang about his being a *chandal*

INDRA:  Chief of gods

KABANDHA: A gandharva who was turned into a demon

DENIZENS: Forest-dwellers

A Rishi

# RISHI MATANG AND SAINT SHABRI

## PROLOGUE

Matang is a highly revered sage. He has been variously eulogized in the scriptures. The story of *Rishi* Matang appears in the Balmiki's *Ramayana* as also in the *Mahabharata*. He was the *guru* (preceptor) of Shabri, a saint and devotee of Lord Rama. It was in the hermitage of sage Matang that Shabri took shelter, observed all austerities, and eventually attained sainthood. And it was in *Rishi* Matang's *ashram* that both Lord Rama and his brother, Lakshmana, met Shabri, and blessed her with *moksha* (deliverance). Sage Matang and saint Shabri are complementary and supplementary to each other; for one glorifies the other. The renown of Matang is all-encompassing, thanks to Shabri, his disciple. Shabri makes the eminence of Matang timeless. And Matang makes Shabri immortal. When one is remembered, the other automatically comes to mind.

## CURTAIN RAISER

My name is Gunadhya. I am actually a celestial being. I came to the earth in the world of mortals as a story-teller. I was the narrator of the tales in Somdeva's famous book *Kathasaritasagara (KATHA-SARITA-SAGARA)*, that is the Ocean of Stories. And I am going to perform the same role of a narrator in telling the story of *Rishi* Matang and his disciple Shabri, who through her devotion elevated herself to the status of a saint. The story of the birth of sage Matang is quite flabbergasting and surprising. And so is the story of Shabri. Though

Matang was born in a Brahman family, he was deemed to be a *chandal* (*dalit* that is low caste, untouchable) because of his enigmatic birth. And equally amazing is the socio-spiritual story of Shabri. She was born in a low-caste family of Bhils. She ran away from her home a day before her marriage, and clandestinely reached *Rishi* Matang's hermitage.

## ACT: ONE

## SCENE: 1

Gunadhya: Matang is a respected, learned ascetic, who hailed from a *chandala* (*dalit*, untouchable) background. But he was a brilliant mind, who attained a very auspicious status by virtue of his *tapas*. The life-story of Matang is quite interesting. His mother was a Brahman, but his father was a barber. The clandestine birth was not known to the Brahman husband, as also to Matang for a long time. As per a legend that appears in the *Mahabharata,* once his Brahaman father sent him to the fields to plough them. He put a donkey to the yoke and ploughed. Soon the foal of an ass got tired and slowed down. He beat the animal with a stick black and blue. The mother of the ass-foal watched this scene with dismay and agony. She told her foal:

Mother Ass: Dear son! Look at that man! I could expect no better treatment from him, for he is no Brahman, but a *chandal*.

Gunadhya: Matang overheard these remarks. He became inquisitive to know as to why the mother-ass spoke those words.

Matang: You seem to be the most intelligent animal. I beg of you to tell me as to how I am a *chandal*, and no Brahman, notwithstanding having been born in a Brahman family.

Mother Ass: Your mother was once inebriated. In that condition she received embraces from a low-born barber. And you were born out of that union. Therefore, you are an offspring of a *chandal*, and not of a Brahman. Go and ask your mother. She will confirm what I have said.

Matang: I thank you for acquainting me with the truth of my life, hitherto hidden from me. In order to obtain elevation to the position of a Brahman, I would undertake severe *tapasya* (penance).

## SCENE: 2

Gunadhya: Matang left his home and went to the mountains. There he engaged himself in stern austerities. His *tapasya* alarmed demigods. Lord Indra descended to the earth.

Indra: Matang! I am pleased with your *tapasya*. Please ask for the boon.

Matang: Please admit me as a Brahman.

Indra: No! That is not possible. You cannot be admitted into the Brahman clan. Please ask for another boon.

Matang: Lord Indra! If you cannot admit me as a Brahman, then I will continue with my penance till you relent.

Gunadhya: Indra disappeared. Matang immersed

himself in still sterner austerities. Though dejected, he did not despair, but proceeded to balance himself on his toe. He continued to do this kind of harsh *tapasya* for many years. Owing to very strenuous *tapas*, Matang was reduced to mere skin and bone. Matang was on the point of falling because of debilitating body, when Indra suddenly appeared, supported and caught him with his hands, and prevented him from falling.

Indra: Matang! What do you want?

Matang: I have already told you about my wish. I want to be admitted as a Brahman.

Indra: I cannot do that. I have already told you.

Matang: Then I would continue with my *tapas*.

Indra: Matang! Since you have inexorably importuned repeatedly, I grant you another boon. I grant you the power of moving about like a bird, and changing your shape at will. And you will be honored and renowned by seers, saints and common people.

Matang: Lord Indra! Since you cannot elevate me as a Brahman, I supplicate to you to grant me another boon.

Indra: What is that?

Matang: I want the Supreme Divine Mother (Devi Parvati) to be born in my family.

Indra: *Tathastu*! Be it so. Your wish is granted. Devi Parvati will be born as your daughter, and she would be named Matangini.

# SCENE: 3

Gunadhya: The Balmiki *Ramayana (Aranya Kanda)* describes the hermitage of sage Matang in detail. While roaming in the forest in search of Sita, Lord Rama and his brother, confronted a demon, named Kabandha. In a fight Kabandha was slain. Kabandha is said to have been a son of goddess Sri. He was originally a Gandharva (a *Vedic* deity). He had a hideous body. His deformity arose, according to a legend, from a quarrel with Indra whom he challenged, and who struck him with his thunderbolt, and drove his head and thighs into his belly. Nevertheless, when he was mortally wounded, he requested Lord Rama to burn his body. And when that was done, he came out of the fire in his real shape as a Gandharva. He counseled Rama as to the conduct of the war against Ravana. Before death, he described the hermitage of Rishi Matang in glowing terms, and sent Rama and Lakshmana to the sage's *ashram.*

Kabandha: (*Extolling the greatness of the ashram of Rishi Matang, he tells Rama)* The flowers of this hermitage are never plucked. Even if they are not plucked, they never fade; they remain fresh always. There is a legend behind this phenomenon. Once the disciples of the sage carried a heavy load of fruits for their *guru.* When they reached near the *ashram,* they were fully exhausted and tired. The drops of their perspiration fell on the plants, and they became flowers.

Lord Rama! before I breathe my last, I want to tell how great *Rishi* Matang is? Once he was engrossed in penance on the Rishyamukha mountain. Bali had a fight with a demon, named Dundubhi. By chance, the blood flowing from the body of the *asura* (demon) fell on the hands of *Rishi* Matang. This annoyed the sage, who cursed Bali that if he ever entered the Rishyamukha mountain again, his head would blow off.

## SCENE: 4

Gunadhya: It was in Sage Matang's *ashram* that Shabri lived. Who is Shabri, and how she arrived there is an interesting story! Her real name was Shramna. She belonged to the "Shabar" caste of Bhil tribe. That is why she was called Shabri.

Her father was the Chief of the Bhil tribe. She was the only daughter of Bhilraj. When she came of age, her father arranged her marriage with a Bhil young man. On the day of her marriage, her father procured several sheep. They were to be slaughtered for the marriage feast. When Shabri came to know of it, she felt aghast. Being a devout, humane and tender-hearted, she believed in non-violence, and the universal goodness for all. She discussed her concerns with her father.

Shabri: Father! Why have you procured so many sheep? And for what purpose?

Bhilraj: Shabri! The tradition has it that before the marriage ceremony, animals are sacrificed. Tomorrow morning before your marriage is solemnized, these sheep will be slaughtered for the marriage feast.

Gunadhya: Having said that, her father went away. But Shabri felt mentally disturbed; she could not sleep during the night. She wanted to save the animals from being killed. She felt guilty, for she thought that it was because of her marriage that so many sheep would be slaughtered. She then decided to run away from home, as this would break the marriage, and the sheep will escape death. So, she slipped away clandestinely much before dawn, and reached sage Matang's *ashram*. In the Dandakaryana forest Rishi Matang was engrossed in *tapasya*. She wanted to serve the sage and other residents of the hermitage, but the people from the Bhil tribe put all kinds of hurdles in her way. But she remained steadfast and undeterred in her mission. She would get up in the wee hours, clean the a*shram*, wean away all the thorns and twigs much before the seer's disciples, saints and other residents of the hermitage woke up. She would meticulously perform this service every day much before the sun rose. For many days her presence was not noticed in the hermitage. None knew as to who cleaned the ashram. One day sage Matang espied her quietly engaged in cleaning the hermitage.

Matang: Who are you Devi?

Shabri: I am Shabri, daughter of Bhilraj. I have run away from home and come to your ashram.

Matang: I am pleased with your devotion. You can stay here forever and immerse yourself in God's *bhakti* (devotion).

Gunadhya: Shabri continued to follow her routine. But she spent most of her time in *tapasya*. After many years, when Matag became old and decrepit, he called Shabri.

Matang: my dear daughter! I have become old. My body has become enfeeble with age. My time to leave this world has come. But before my death I want to bless you. Please tell me what do you want!

Shabri: Reverend sage! You are my father, my mentor, my guru. I am here and alive because of your blessings. You willingly faced ostracism for adopting a low caste as your disciple. How would I live in your absence? Please take me to the heaven along with you.

Matang: Shabri! You are like my daughter. Please do not talk like this. In my absence, you have to take care of the *ashram*. I assure you that you will be adequately compensated for your pious actions. One day Lord Rama, an incarnation of Lord Vishnu, will come to the hermitage to meet you. On that day your blessed soul will get *moksha* (deliverance).

## SCENE: 5

Gunadhya: *Rishi* Matang died and took "samadhi." From that day onwards, Shabri, believing the prophecy of his *guru,* would go to the forest every day, and collect "ber" (berries) for Lord Rama. She always tasted the berries; the sweet berries she kept in the basket, and the sour she threw away. Owing to her *tapasya*, she raised herself to the rank of a saint.

One day, she went to a mountain pool to fetch water. Close by a sage was immersed in *tapasya*. When he saw an untouchable woman taking water from the pool, he lost the cool of his mind. He threw a stone at her. The stone hurt Shabri. She started bleeding. The blood from her body spilled into the fresh -water pool. The water of the pool turned blood-red.

Rishi: You sinful woman! What have you done? Your blood has made the pool- water impious. This pool was the only source of drinking water for the people living in the surrounding areas. And you have profaned it. Now, I will have to make efforts to purify it.

Gunadhya: Shabri returned to the *ashram* crying. However, she did not show any anger against the *Rishi*. The *Rishi* did his best to restore the water to its original purity, but he failed in his efforts. At that time, Lord Rama, along with his brother, came there. They were on their way to the hermitage of sage Matang. The common people who were feeling a lot of hardship for want of fresh water, approached Lord Rama. They narrated the entire happening to him.

Denizens: Lord Rama! We have heard that with the touch of your feet, you restored Devi Ahalya (wife of sage Gautama) from a stone to a celestial woman. Therefore, we supplicate to you to touch with your feet the water of this pool, and restore it to its original purity and piety.

Lord Rama: Sage! Please tell me, what has happened?

Rishi: Shabri, the low-caste woman spoiled the water of the pool, by throwing her blood into it.

Lord Rama: Sage! You have committed a sin. You are guilty. Your action is unworthy of you. In fact, you have abused me and bled my heart by hurting and abusing Shabri, my devotee. When somebody hurts my *bhakt* (devotee), he actually hurts me. And I do not forgive that sinner. (*Addressing the denizens*): If you want the water to be purified, please bring Shabri here.

Gunadhya: The common people rushed to fetch

Shabri. When Shabri heard that his *Prabhu* (God, Lord Rama) has arrived, she came running. The dust raised by the feet of Shabri, fell into the water pool. The water immediately turned fresh, as shimmering and waving in the zephyr as before. Then Lord Rama, along with his brother, ultimately reached the *ashram* of sage Matang. Thus, Lord Rama gave "*darshan*" to her *bhakt* (devotee).

## SCENE: 6

Gunadhya: Shabri brought Lord Rama and his brother to her *ashram*. She had spread flowers on the pathway to her hermitage. Immediately she took berries out of the basket, which as a daily routine she had plucked from the forest, tasted them; those sweet she had put in the basket, and those sour she had discarded. She offered those berries to Lord Rama. She did not know that offering to God must not be tasted. But the ecstatic soul of a devotee does not care about the social norms.

Shabri: There are hundreds of exalted *yogis* and saints waiting for your *darshan*, but you, Lord Rama, preferred to visit a low-born ordinary devotee, living in a humble hut.

Lord Rama: I only see the devotion of a devotee, irrespective of the fact whether he or she lives in a palace, or in a humble hut. Whether a person comes from the upper or the lower caste, I don't care; nor do I bother whether he or she is learned, erudite or ignorant. I only see true *bhakti* (devotion).

Shabri: Lord Rama! I do not have anything to offer other than my heart. But here are some berries. May it please you my Lord to taste them.

Gunadhya: Shabri offered the fruit she had meticulously collected. As Rama tasted them, he offered some to his younger brother, Lakshmana.

Lakshmana: Brother! Shabri had already tasted the berries. Therefore, they are unworthy of eating.

Lord Rama: Lakshmana! Of the varied types of fruits and food I have tasted, nothing could equal these berries, since they have been offered with sincere devotion. When you taste them, then alone will you know their worth. Whosoever offers fruit, flower or water, with love, I partake in it with great joy. In *bhakti*, the deities do not find any fault, and such offerings are never unworthy.

Gunadhya: Lakshmana did not taste the berries, given to him by Rama. He threw them away. Scriptures have it that when in the Rama-Ravana battle, Lakshmana was hit by *shakti* and he became unconscious, a concoction made of berries revived him.

Lord Rama: I notice the *donas* (bowls) in which you offered berries to me. They are made out of leaves of a tree. I bless the tree that its leaves will naturally grow in the shape of a bowl. I bless you Shabri, and grant you *moksha* (deliverance).

## EPILOGUE

The story of Rishi Matang and Shabri has a great socio-political and religious message. The moral of the story is that the worth of a human being has to be judged by "karma" (actions), by what he or she makes himself or herself, and not by birth. Caste is determined by birth, and the birth is something on which a person has no control. There is an apocryphal line attributed to Karna in the *Mahabharata*: "My birth in a family is under the control of the book of fate, but I myself control my qualities as a human being."

The significance is obvious. A person may be born in a lowly family, but through efforts, determination and cultivation of virtues, he may rise in life and become "somebody." Matang –and- Shabri -story explodes the myth of hierarchical social order. Through their "karma" (actions), they raised themselves to a high pedestal of life. The analogy applies to Karna also, who became a great hero, the only match of invincible Arjuna, though he was supposed to be the son of an ordinary charioteer. Vidura too was born of a "sudra" slave woman. But owing to his righteous actions, he came to be called a "Mahatma": and the "wisest of the wise."

There is no gainsaying the fact that there are extraordinary possibilities in ordinary people. Actions determine the status of a person, and not his birth or caste. Rishi Matang and saint Shabri teach us the ethics of life.

*****

# 4.RISHYSA-SHRINGA AND KING LOMA-PADA

## DRAMATIS PERSONAE

GUNADHYA: The narrator of the story

VIBHANDAKA: A sage, son of *Rishi* Kashyapa

RISHYA-SHRINGA: A renowned seer; Son of Vibhandaka

LOMA-PADA: King of Anga

SOOTHSAYER: who foretells future

SUMANTRA: The charioteer of king Dasharatha

AN OLD COURTESAN: The chief courtesan

A young beautiful courtesan who succeeds in enticing Rishya-shringa

# RISHYA –SHRINGA AND KING LOMA – PADA

## PROLOGUE

It was the best of times when India in a hoary past was more prosperous socially, culturally, religiously and spiritually. It was an altogether different Bharat. The towns and villages were sparsely populated. They were encompassed by lush-green forests and valley-glades. Woods were lovely, dark and deep, and through them flowed many a sacred river and fresh water brooks. In the woodland, on the banks of rivers and rivulets, mountain pools and lakes, were situated *ashrams* of seers and saints. These hermitages were interspersed in every nook and corner of the country. They were the temples of learning, of religious rituals. The disciples of the sages and other saints sojourned there. The common populace paid due deference to the sages and the *ashrams* were regarded as sacred institutions which imparted education appertaining temporal and spiritual knowledge. That knowledge is embedded in our scriptures and epics.

A reading of the scriptures as also of the epics, the *Ramayana* and the *Mahabharata*, substantiates the fact that in the v*edic* and the post-*vedic* era, demigods and *apsaras* (celestial nymphs, danseuse) travelled to and fro the heaven and the earth. Sometimes they traversed the world of mortals on their own volition, and sometimes were sent on some specific mission. Stories of gods and celestial nymphs descending on the earth are interspersed in the *Puranas* and in other scriptures as also in the classical literature. Menaka, a celestial nymph, was dispatched by Lord Indra to break the penance of sage Viswamitra. *Rishi* Viswamitra fell in love with her, and out of their union was born Shakuntla, who transformed the course of history for the future generations of India.

Similarly, *apsara* Urvashi roused the passions of sage Vibhandaka, who let his seminal fluid flow into a stream, which impregnated a deer. And eventually Rishya-Shringa was born who created a new history.

## CURTAIN RAISER

My name is Gunadhya. I am a celestial being. I came to the earth in the world of mortals as a story-teller. I was the narrator of tales in Somdeva's famous book *Kathasaritasagara (KATHA-SARITA-SAGARA)*, that is the Ocean of Stories. And I am going to perform the same role of a narrator in telling the story of Rishya-shringa and Lomapada, a monarch of Anga, and a friend of Dasharatha, king of Ayodhya. The story dilates on the marriage of Rishya-shringa, a staunch celibate, with Santa, daughter of Loma-Pada.

There was a *Rishi*, named Vibhandaka. He was a son of sage Kashyapa. Once while washing his mouth at the bank of a river, he beheld the celestial nymph, Urvashi. Vibhandaka was a renowned sage engrossed in austerities. Lord Indra invariasbly dreaded such seers. So, he wanted to discredit Vibhandaka. Form this sinister act, he sent *apsara* Urvashi to tempt and beguile the sage. The sight of the most beautiful and attractive celestial nymph sexually excited Vibhandaka to such an aextent that his seminal fluid fell into the river. Downstream a female deer was drinking water. She lapped up the sage's seminal fluid along with the water. In fact, this female deer was another *apsara*, cursed by Lord Brahma to be born as a deer. The impregnated deer gave birth to a son. Since there was a horn on his fore-head, he was named Shringi. After the birth of Shringi, the nymph was freed of the curse. As sage Vibhandaka was deluded by an *apsara*, he developed hatred for the woman-folk in general. Vibhandaka built his hermitage at an isolated place deep into the forest, where he brought up his son away from all men and women, and made him a staunch celibate.

## ACT: ONE

## SCENE: 1

Gunadhya: The story of Rishya-shringa appears in the *Ramayana*, as also in the *Mahabharata*. In the *Ramayana* the story is narrated by Sumantra, the charioteer of king Dasharatha. However, a more detailed version is depicted in the *Mahabharata*.

Rishya-shringa literally means "the deer- horned." He is a renowned hermit, the son of *Rishi* Vibhandaka, and the grand-son of sage Kashyapa (father of Vibhandaka). Sage Kashyapa is one of the *saptrishis* (the seven famed *Rishis*), considered to be the authors of many hymns and verses in the *Rig Veda*.

The *Mahabharata* story has it that sage Vibhandka spent his days in penance and austerities. He followed a daily routine of going to a river that flowed close to his *ashram,* washed his mouth in its waters and took a morning bath. One day while he was washing his mouth in the waters, he beheld Urvashi, the celestial nymph. The incomparable beauty of the *apsara* roused his passions, whereupon came out his seminal fluid. A hind lapped it up along with the water she was drinking. Since the seed of Vibhandaka never failed in causing birth, the hind became pregnant. Eventually, she gave birth to a son with a horn on his forehead. The same hind (female deer) was a *devkanya* (a daughter of the gods), and had been transferred into a hind by Brahma who declared that "when she gave birth to a sage, she would be restored to her original shape." Since the child was born with a horn on his forehead, he was named as Rishya-shringa. He is known to be "foremost among Rishis."

Vibhandaka: I am ashamed of myself; for I indulged in a scurrilous and wanton act by yielding to passions; the momentary lapse gnaws at the esteem and credibility of me-like saint, leading a life of abstinence. But now I will make amends for my slip up. I will bring up my son Rishya-shringa in a secluded place, deep in the forest, away from men and women and hum-drum routine of the common world. I will bring him up as a strict Brahamachari (celibate). He will lead his life in the company of only his father. In the hermitage, there will be only two persons, my son and I, and no third person. He will never see, or interact, with women.

Gunadhya: Growing up in the hermitage, situated deep in the forest, Rishya-shringa was ignorant of the outside world, and of the very existence of beings other than his father and himself. He had never seen a woman, and did not know that such a creature existed. He believed that everyone in the world was exactly like him and his father.

During this time the neighbouring kingdom of

Anga was ruled by Loma-pada. The monarch had displeased the gods by uttering a falsehood to a Brahman. Resultantly, he was avoided by all the priests; for none would serve in a kingdom where falsehood reigned supreme. Therefore, he had no officiating priest, and could not perform any sacrifice (*yagya*). Since the gods, including Lord Indra did not get sacrificial offerings owing to non-performance of sacrifices, they turned against king Loma-pada. Thus, displeased Indra punished Loma-pada by withholding rains from his kingdom which suffered from a severe drought. King Loma-pada was advised by his ministers to consult a famous soothsayer to tide over the problems.

Loma-pada: (*The king summoned a well-known soothsayer of the kingdom for consultation*) Sire! You are very wise and knowledgeable. You have the vision to foretell future. The kingdom is facing severe famine. I seek your counsel as to by what means the sufferings of the common populace can be mitigated.

Soothsayer: O king! I visualize that the end of the natural calamity that has befallen the kingdom, lies with sage Rishya-shringa. As long as Rishya-shringa continues to remain chaste, so long would the drought prevail. Rishya-shringa is the foremost among the brahamcharis (celibates). He lives with his father, *Rishi* Vibhandaka. The rain shall fall when he comes to your kingdom. But his father will not allow him to leave the forest. I advise you to send some lovely courtesan to the hermitage of Vibhandaka, where Risya-shringa lives. She will use all stratagems and ploys to bewitch and entice Rishya-shringa and bring him here. The moment he sets foot on the land of Anga, the required rain will fall.

Loma-pada: Chief courtesan! I entrust this onerous errand to you. Go to the *ashram* of Vibhandaka, lure the sage's son, Rishya-shringa, and bring him here.

Gunadhya: The chief courtesan hesitated to do the bidding of the king. On the one hand she did not want to annoy the king and wanted the drought to end, on the other hand she knew that her job was fraught with perilous consequences. She was apprehensive of the wrath of *Rishi* Vibhandaka, lest he should punish her with a curse. Therefore, she was caught between the devil and the deep sea. Nevertheless, she mustered courage to speak to the king.

Chief Courtesan: O king! I am ready to carry out your orders. But I am in a catch-22 situation. To tempt Rishya-shringa and persuade him to come to the kingdom, is replete with dangerous ramifications. In case sage Vibhandaka gets an inkling of our plan to abduct his son, he will severely punish the delinquent with a curse.

Loma-pada: Please worry you not! You will not be alone in the task. You can entrust the task to your young and beautiful daughter. She is intelligent enough to accomplish the mission. She will take some other young attractive courtesans as her companions with her. As far as *Rishi* Vibhandaka is concerned, I will make adequate arrangements to protect you and your daughter from the anger of the sage. I assure you that I will take full care of all of you. You and your fellow courtesans shall be handsomely rewarded for the service.

## SCENE: 2

Gunadhya: The old courtesan with her fair daughter in tow undertook the seduction of Rishsya-shringa. The king had a boat filled with all kinds of luxuries, dainty food items, tasty drinks, perfumes, costly jewels, etc. On the boat was erected a replica of a hermitage, adorned with fruit-laden trees and bushes on which bloomed fragrant flowers. The boat carried the young daughter of the courtesan to a point not far from Rishsya-shringa's hermitage. She disguised herself as a hermit, and waited for sage Vibhandaka to be out of home. As soon as she found out that Vibhandaka had gone out, and that Rishya-shringa was alone in the *ashram* (hermitage), she rowed the boat to the closest vicinity of Rishyaa-shringa's hermitage.

Young Courtesan: (*Greeting Rishya-shringa*) Sir! I am sure your holiness is engaged in religious duties with utmost devotion. I find that in this lush-green forest there is no dearth of fruits and roots for you and for other forest-dwellers. I hope you must be doing fine in your spiritual pursuits and religious duties.

Gunadhya: Rishya-shringa had never seen such a handsome creature before. He was awe-struck by the bewitching beauty of the young girl, disguised as she was in the garb of a hermit. Rishya-shringa mistook her to be a hermit.

Rishya-shringa: Young saint! I greet and welcome you. You are glowing and dazzling like a luminous halo as if you are a mass of luster. I pay my obeisance to you. You are perhaps some god in disguise who has come to visit me. Saint! Where is your hermitage? I have never seen before as enthralling a hermit as you.

Young courtesan: O grandson of Rishi Kashyapa! My hermitage is on the other side of the hill, quite far off from this place.

Gunadhya: The young courtesan offered Rishya-shringa palatable sweets and fruits, which he had never tasted before. She also offered him flavored drinks. She gave him garlands made of fragrant and sweet-smelling flowers. In this interaction, she deliberately touched her body with that of Rishya-shringa, and clasped him in her arms repeatedly. The touch of a young beautiful girl excited Rishya-shringa, and a strange kind of sensation passed through his corporeal frame. He could not understand as to what is happening; nor could he realize and recognize as to who she was and for what purpose she had come. After she took leave, he became lovelorn, and became oblivious of his daily religious functions and rituals.

## SCENE: 3

Vibhandaka: (*When Vibhandaka returned he found his son a changed person. He had not lit the fire of sacrifice, nor milked the cows*). Son! What has happened to you in my absence? You are not your original self. You have neither lit the fire for the sacrifice, nor milked the kines. What is the matter, tell me?

Rishya-shringa: Father! While you were away, a young hermit came here. He was a young brahamchari with a mass of hair parted in the center, fully accoutered in lustrous garb, a rosary in hand, and was extremely handsome. Innumerable ornaments embellished his body. His beauty was so captivating that it gladdened my heart. He taught me a unique form of religious worship by repeatedly embracing me. His hug was highly delightful. He left the hermitage a little while ago before you came. I want to be in his company all the time. O father! let me this very moment go to him.

Vibhandaka: (*Suspecting some foul play, the sage warns his son*) Son! Fiends in different disguises strove the forest to tempt hermits to their undoing. The person who visited you in my absence cannot be a hermit. He must be some *rakshasa* (demon) disguised in wondrous beautiful form with an evil mind to beguile you. Such demons cause hurdles in the religious practices of saints and obstruct them from doing *tapasya* (penance). Beware of them. They are dangerous. Avoid their company in future.

## SCENE: 4

Gunadhya: A few days later, Vibhandaka was again absent from his hermitage. He had gone to the forest to collect wood for the sacrifice. Finding the time opportune for the fulfillment of her mission, the young courtesan returned, and attempted to persuade Rishya-shringa to accompany her to her hermitage. As soon the young sage saw her, he came running to her and hugged her.

Rishya-shringa: My father has warned me against you. He said that fiends in various garbs wandered in the forest to hoodwink the hermits, so that they neglect their religious duties. But your company gives me intense pleasure, a kind of sensational thrill, hitherto unknown to me. I want to be in your company all the time.

Young courtesan: I also rejoice in your company. Come and board my boat. I will take you to my hermitage.

Gunadhya: The courtesan was glad that she had accomplished her task so easily. She led the sage to her boat. Once inside the boat, Rishsya-shringa was entertained by the young courtesan with sumptuous eatables and flavorsome drinks. There were many other beautiful women inside the boat. Rishya-shringa had never seen such beautiful women, and so large in number, before. All of them enticed him with their womanly wanton gestures.

The boat sailed, and the lad was eventually clandestinely taken to the kingdom of Anga, where he was housed by king Loma-pada in the palace in the apartment meant for women.

## SCENE: 5

Gunadhya: The king subsequently had his daughter Shanta married to Rishya-shringa. Shanta was the daughter of Dasharatha, king of Ayodhya. Since Ayodhya and Anga were two contiguous states, there was close friendship between the two kings, Dasharatha and Lomapada. Lomapada had adopted and brought up Shanta as his daughter. As soon as the marriage was consummated, the dry spell ended, the rain fell in abundance. The land of Anga was saved from famine.

Meanwhile, when sage Vibhandaka returned from the forest, he did not find his son in the hermitage. Through his *yogic* power, he could visualize as to what had happened. He became furious. He scurried post-haste towards Anga to punish monarch Loma-pada for his serious dereliction.

Loma-pada: (*When the monarch of Anga learnt of Vibhadaka's fury, he planned a strategy to appease the sage*). Guards and messengers! Please line up hundreds of cows all along the entire route through which the sage is expected to pass. Tell him repeatedly, after every short distance, that all these cattle belong to him and that these are his property. Also tell him that, in fact, the entire kingdom belongs to him, and that the inhabitants of Anga are his subjects.

Gunadhya: The ruse worked well with the sage. He was duly pacified, especially when he was told that the king had his daughter, Shanta, married to his son. Whatever little anger remained completely vanished when in the palace he saw his son seated on the throne with his beautiful wife, Shanta.

Vibhandaka: Rishya-shringa! I bless you and your wife. After you have performed the duties and errands agreeable to the king, and as soon as Shanta gives birth to a son, you will return to the forest.

Gunadhya: After a son was born to Rishya-shringa, he followed the instructions of his father, and returned to his hermitage with his wife, Shanta. In fact, Shanta was the daughter of king Dasharatha, but she was adopted and brought up by Loma-pada, the king of Anga.

## SCENE: 6

Sumantra: (*Dasharatha did not have any child. His ministers advised him to perform Ashwa-medha yagya*). Rajan! I have been your charioteer for a very long time. I narrate to you the legend of *Rishi* Rishya-shringa. It has been foretold that the *Aswamedha* sacrifice being contemplated by you shall be performed by Rishya-shringa. Therefore, please appoint the sage to perform the proposed *yagya* (sacrifice) that would bless you with children.

Gunadhya: It was Rishya-shringa who performed the sacrifice, and the *charu* (sacrificial offering) was given to the three queens, who ate them and eventually gave birth to four sons, Rama, Bharat, Lakshman, and Shatrughan.

## EPILOGUE

The significance of the story of Rishya-shringa lies in the "ceremonial marriage." It is symptomatic of the "fertility ritual," which is especially efficacious in bringing about the desired result. The efficacy of the rite appears to have been enhanced by the strict observance of the rule of chastity by the protagonist. The hallmark of Rishya-shringa's personality is his woodland life, and the distinguished quality of his child-like innocence.

A drought falls on the kingdom of Anga, and will persist until a young man abandons the chastity in which he has been reared. When the boy has been sought, found, tempted and won, and his marriage with the king's daughter consummated, the dry spell is broken and the refreshing rain comes. King Loma-pada is punished for committing a sin against the social, religious and ethical norms. It is only Rishya-shringa who can help bring the required rain to the parched land, for water is the main source of fertility. Rishya-shringa, the hero, the harbinger of salvation, is lured and initiated into the magnificent act of fertilization through water. It is in search for the fertilization of land that Loma-pada sends his questers who, interestingly enough, reach their destination by a similar mode of transportation, that is a boat cruising along water, the symbol of regeneration. Rishsya-shringa, through his feat, brings joy to the parched hearts of the suffering people.

*****

# 5. RISHI MARKANDEYA WHO DEFEATED DEATH

## DRAMATIS PEROSNAE

GUNADHYA: The Narrator of the story

MRIKANDU: A sage, and father of Markandeya

MARUDVATI: Wife of *Rishi* Mrikandu, and mother of Markandeya

MARKANDEYA: An ancient seer, son of sage Mrikandu

SHIVA: A Supreme God, Mahadeva, Rudra

YAMA: God of death

YAMDOOTS: Messengers of god of death

DEMIGODS

# RISHI MARKANDEYA WHO DEFEATED DEATH

## PROLOGUE

Markandeya is an ancient sage. He hails from the clan of Rishi Bhrigu. He is the reputed author of the *Markandeya Purana*, which commences with the story of birds that were acquainted with what is right and what is wrong. This *Purana*, narrated by Markandeya, contains stories of fabulous birds, well versed in the *Vedas*. The birds exhibit their deep knowledge while answering the questions of *Rishi* Gemini. The discussion virtually becomes a dialogue between the two seers, Markandeya and Gemini. *Markandeya Purana* is totally different from all other *Puranas*. It has little of religious tone. It does not have much of prayers and invocations to any deity. Unlike many other *Puranas*, it does not deal with precepts, ceremonial or moral. Its cardinal feature is narrative; and it presents an uninterrupted succession of legends.

Markandeya, the celebrated sage, was a devotee of both Lord Vishnu and Lord Shiva. A number of legends about this saint are mentioned in holy scriptures; especially in several chapters in the *Bhagvat Purana*, which are dedicated to his conversations. *Rishi* Markandeya is also prominently mentioned in the *Mahabharata*.

Nevertheless, the legend of sage Markandeya is remarkable for his devotion to Lord Shiva and his ultimate defeat of Yama, the god of death. The legend has it that he was born with only a short life of sixteen years. But owing to his *tapasya* (penance), he defied god of death, and got a boon from Lord

Shiva for long life and eternal youth. He was thus a "Dirghayu," (the long lived). Since sage Markandeya defeated Yama (god of death), he was called "kalakal", that is "Death of Death." Verily, for everything in the world, we need blessings of the Supreme Being. And when the Supreme Lord blesses, one can achieve those heights which initially appear to be difficult and hazardous. This is what the legend of saint Markandeya propounds; that a person may be born with a long or short life according to his *karmas* (actions), but through unflinching *bhakti* (devotion), he can alter his fate and prolong his life span.

## CURTAIN RAISER

My name is Gunadhya. I am a celestial being. I came to the earth in the world of mortals as a story-teller. I was the narrator of tales in Somdeva's famous book *Kathasaritasagara (KATHA –SARITA-SAGARA)*, that is the Ocean of Stories. And I am going to perform the same role of a narrator in telling the story of Markandeya. Markandeya was born with a short span of life. But with his resolute mind and steadfast devotion, he pleased Lord Shiva, who metamorphosed his short life into a long life, and also granted him a boon of eternal youth. Lord Shiva got so much annoyed with Yama for daring to take the life of his devotee, engrossed in his *bhakti* that Rudra severely punished him. Eventually, at the request of demigods, he forgave Yamraj. From that day onwards, Rudra (that is Lord Shiva), got the name of KALANTAKA (the Ender of Death); for he stopped the god of death from taking the life of his devotee, notwithstanding the fact that the allotted life-span of Markandeya was up, and his life was destined to be taken away by Yama.

## ACT: ONE

## SCENE: 1

Gunadhya: The legend has it that Rishi Mrikandu and his wife, Marudvati, were childless. They were both devotees of Lord Shiva. They lived a life of simplicity and spirituality in their *ashram*. One day, it so happened, that a cowherd Gopa, brought home the cows at sun-set after grazing them. Mrikandu and his wife saw a cow-calf jumping and tip-toeing playfully, repeatedly nudging his mother. The mother also caressed her calf affectionately. Seeing the calf in such a playful mood, Marudvati felt the want of a child.

Marudvati: A child! that is what is missing in our life.

Mrikandu: You are right, Marudvati! Life is incomplete without a child. We should worship Lord Shiva, and beseech him to bless us with a son.

Gunadhya: Both the hermit and his wife were staunch devotees of Lord Shiva. They decided to perform intense *tapas* (penance). Shiva manifested himself to the couple.

Lord Shiva: I am pleased with your *bhakti* and *tapasya*. Ask for any boon, you desire.

Mrikandu: O Lord! I have no child. Please grant me a son.

Lord Shiva: You are not destined to have a progeny. But since you have pleased me with your devotion, I will grant your wish. What kind of a child do you want? You have to choose one of the two options. Do you want evil-natured, dull-witted son with a long life, or a virtuous, wise and pious son with a short life of only sixteen years?

Gunadhya: The couple ruminated over the matter and ultimately chose the second option.

Mrikandu: Lord! We do not want a worthless son. We supplicate to you to bless us with a son, who is wise, righteous and upright, even if he has a short span of life.

Lord Shiva: *Tathastu*! Be it so.

## SCENE: 2

Gunadhya: After some time Marudvati conceived and gave birth to a son, who was named Markandeya. Mrikandu sent his son to a hermitage for education, temporal and spiritual. He studied in a seer's *ashram* for fifteen years, where he imbibed the knowledge embedded in the scriptures. Even in boyhood he had mastered all the *Vedas*. He was a gifted child; and an obedient son. Owing to his pleasant behavior, he endeared himself to everybody; the common populace loved him dearly. After the completion of his studies in a *Gurukul* (school), Markandeya returned home.

As soon as the sixteenth year of Markandeya's life commenced, his parents plunged into gloom, for they knew that the end of life of their son was near.

Markandeya: Father! You are looking morose and woeful. What the matter is? Have I done something wrong that has made you despondent and depressed?

Mrikandu: No, son! You have done no wrong. You cannot do anything unrighteous and unethical.

Markandeya: No, there is certainly something which has made you dismal and doleful. You are concealing some secret from me. Please tell me all, if you love me.

Mrikandu: O, my son! You were born because of the blessings of Lord Shiva. But He destined you to live on the earth only for sixteen years. As the time of your death is coming near, we cannot withstand the unforeseen grief and torment.

Markandeya: Father! One should not dread death. One who is born is foreordained to die. But worry you not! I will vanquish death. I will undertake severe penance to please Lord Shiva. I need your blessings; the blessings of my parents will help me defeat death.

## SCENE: 3

Gunadhya: After seeking the permission and blessings of his parents, Markandeya embarked on *tapasya*. He went to a forest, and there he started worshipping Lord Shiva in the form of a *lingam*. He immersed himself in *tapasya* unflinchingly for one year, chanting "*Om Namah Shivaye*." At last, the death-day arrived. *Yamdoots*, the messengers of death, came to take him away. But immersed as he was in Lord Shiva's *tapasya*, the moment the *yamdoots* came closer to him, a radiation emerged from the *shiva-lingam*, which hurled them far away. The *Yamdoots* returned empty handed, and informed Yama about what had happened.

Yamdoots: lord! We could not take Markandeya's life. He was sitting in front of a *Shiva-lingam*, and chanting mantras, especially "Maha Mrituyanjaya Mantra, "the life-protecting and life-giving chant. The moment we tried to catch hold of him to bring him here, a dazzling radiation emerged, which heaved and hurled us far away from our victim.

Yama:  In that case, I will go myself to take his life as his time is up.

Gunadhya: Yama came himself riding a buffalo. He had a long rope in his hand. He was surprised to see that Markandeya was power packed. He hesitated to touch him.

## SCENE: 4

Yamraj: Markandeya! your time on this earth is up. I have come to take your life.

Markandeya: (*The sage opened his eyes, and saw Yama riding on the back of a buffalo. But he was not scared; nor was he panicked*). Yama! Don't you see I am engrossed in Shiva's *bhakti*? You cannot take my life away. I am reciting "Maha Mritunjaya Mantra," Lord Shiva will protect me.

Gunadhya: Markandeya then hugged the *shiva-lingam* with both arms.

Yama: Markandeya! Leave the *Shiva-lingam*, and come with me, otherwise I will have to use force.

Markandeya: No! You cannot take me away.

Gunadhyaa: The brazen audacity infuriated Yama He threw his rope with the loop; the rope encircled Markandeya's neck as also the *shiva-lingam* which the hermit was clutching. The god of death attempted to pull Markandeya and drag him along with the *lingam.* Suddenly, there was a big bang and a flash of light. The *lingam* split into two, and out of it, manifested Rudra, the fierce form of Mahadeva with a *Trishul* (trident) in his hand.

Lord Shiva: (*Angrily roaring at Yamraj*). How dare you drag my devotee, when he is fully immersed in my *bhakti*. You are guilty of transgression, for along with my devotee, you also attempted to heave *lingam,* my symbolic manifestation on the earth. You have thus committed a blasphemous and profane act. Therefore, you need to be punished severely for this impudence.

Gunadhya: Lord Shiva pushed Yama aside, and killed him with his trident, and thus saved his young devotee, Markandeya.

Demigods: Lord Shiva! Take mercy on Yama. Of course, he has committed a sacrilege. We beseech you to forgive him for his dereliction.

Gunadhya: Lord Shiva acquiesced. He restored Yama to life.

Yama: Shiva! I am your servant. It was you, my lord, who allotted only sixteen years of life to Markandeya. Since it was enjoined on me to take away life of a man when his time on the earth is up, I did my unpleasant duty assigned to me by you. I am highly grateful to you for condoning my remissness. I will now leave for my abode.

## SCENE: 5

Gunadhya: After Yama left, Mahadeva turned towards Markandeya to bless him.

Lord Shiva: Markandeya! I am pleased with your devotion. Hence onwards you will be known as "Mritunjaya "(one who wins death), and KALAKAL (Death of Death). The "Maha Mritunjaya Mantra "that you recited to please me and win over the death, will be your bountiful contribution to the well-being of mankind. In future whosoever chants this mantra will be free from all ills, sufferings, trials and tribulations. You will be remembered and respected for Mritunjaya Mantra.

Since I am pleased with your piety, I bless you with deathlessness. Every desire of yours will be fulfilled. You will never grow old; you will always remain young. You will lead a virtuous life till the end of the world. Omniscience will be your asset.

Gunadhya: Markandeya was a silent spectator to all that was happening in front of his eyes. He remained dumbstruck. Suddenly he realized his *Ishtdev* (Benign God) had showered blessings on him. He prostrated before Shiva, because it was owing to Rudra's benediction that he could conquer death. Blessed thus with long life, Markandeya then returned home to his parents.

## EPILOGUE

In every religion there are mantras, hymns, chants that the followers recite to solicit solace and comfort.

The Hindu religion is no exception. There are two mantras which have held significance from eons. One is the Gayatri Mantra, which sage Viswamitra gave to the world. And the other is Maha Mritunjaya Mantra which Rishi Markandeya gave to the human beings for their well-being. Explained below is the Mritunjaya mantra, its meaning, interpretation and import.

*Om tryambakam yajamahe sugandhim pushti-vardhanam*

*Urvarukam iva bandhanan mrityor muksiya ma mritat*

**Aum**: A sacred syllable

**tryambakam***:* The three-eyed (Rudra, that is Shiva): *tri*: three; *ambaka*: eye

**yajamahe**: We worship, we sacrifice

**sugandhim**: the fragrant, the virtuous, the Supreme being

**pushti + vardhanan**: the bestower of nourishment, wealth, perfection: *pushti*: nourishment, increase in wealth; vardhanan: increase. growth

**urvarukam**: fruit, a kind of cucumber; **iva**: as (written together as *urvarukamiva*)

**bandhanan**: from bondage (bandhanan here means from the "stem."); Fruit is a simile for the worshipper / devotee being released from the bondage of death.

*mrityo*r: from death

*mukshiya*: may I be freed, released

*ma mritat*: *ma* (not) from immortality (*amritat*)

(I worship that fragrant Shiva; the one who nourishes all living entities. May He help us sever our bondage with *samsasra* (world) by making us realize that we are never separated from our immortal nature).

According to a legend Markandeya was the only saint who knew this mantra. The mantra is also called the Rudra mantra, referring to the fierce aspect of Shiva, the Tryambakam, alluding to Shiva's three eyes. It is sometimes known as "Mrit-Sanjivinimantra, because it has the life-restoring power, as practiced by primordial sage Shukracharya after he had completed an exhaustive period of austerities. The patron deity of the mantra is Rudra, that is Shiva in his fiercest and the most destructive form. In the *Vedas,* it finds its place in three texts, *Rig Veda, Yajur Veda* and the *Atharva Veda.*

It is propounded that this mantra is beneficial for mental, emotional and physical health. It is, in fact, a *moksha* mantra, which bestows longevity and immortality. The mantra is addressed to Shiva for warding off untimely death.

The literal translation of the mantra is "victory over death:" Mritunjaya means one who vanquishes and achieves victory over death. The Maha Mritunjaya Mantra is a boon to humanity, and a panacea for all forms of ailments, temporal and spiritual.

*****

# 6.ASHTA-VAKRA: THE LEARNED SEER IN RAJA JANAK'S COURT

## DRAMATIS PERSONAE

GUNADHYA: The narrator of the story

ASHTAVAKRA: A renowned sage with eight deformities / bends in his body

KAHODA: Father of Ashtavakra

SUJATA: Mother of Ashtavakra

UDDALAKA: Maternal grand-father of Ashtavakra

SHVETAKETU: Maternal uncle of Ashtavakra

JANAKA: King of Mithila, and father-in-law of Lord Rama

VANDIN: A learned Brahman who was defeated in debate by Ashtavakra

Monks

Helper

# ASHTA-VAKRA: THE LEARNED SEER IN RAJA JANAK'S COURT

## PROLOGUE

When we are surrounded by external problems, we become despondent. This despondency, this despair, gradually turns into anguish and distress. And for this uncomfortable situation we generally blame others, and suffer pain. But there are individuals who metamorphose plight into a pragmatic and expedient opportunity to do things positive. The case in point is that of *Rishi* Ashta-vakra, who turned physical deformity into a life of spiritual advancement and intellectual reckoning. Verily, one who has a strong mind can mould the world to himself. This is what Ashtavakra did. He became well-versed in the *Vedas* and other scriptures. And owing to his learning, he won the *Shastraarth* – (a verbal contest on the meaning and interpretation of scriptures) competition in the court of Janaka, king of Mithila, and father in-law of Lord Rama.

As is implied in his name, the sage had "ashta "(eight) "vakra "(deformities) in his body. He was cursed by his father, Kahoda, to be born with eight bends in his body as he had humiliated him. But through his sagacity, he transformed this curse into a boon. And thus, he played his onerous part in the well-being of the mankind.

As mentioned earlier in the story of sage Matang and saint Shabri, which appears in the *Aranya Kand* of the *Ramayana*, the demon Kabandha tells Lord Rama that he was actually a Gandharva. But *Rishi* Ashtavakra cursed him to become a demon when he laughed at him on seeing his deformed body. When Kabandha apologized for his impudence, sage Ashtavakra told him that he would be freed from the curse when Lord Rama comes to visit Shabri in the *ashram* of sage Matang.

Ashtavakra is also cited in the *Yuddha Kand* of Valmiki's *Ramayana*. When Raja Dashrath comes to see Rama from heaven after the war, he tells Lord Rama:

"O son! I have been conveyed across (redeemed) by you, who is a deserving son and a great being, like the virtuous Brahman Kahoda, who was redeemed, by his son Ashtavakra.

## CURTAIN RAISER

My name is Gunadhya. I am a celestial being. I came to the earth in the world of mortals as a story-teller. I was the narrator of tales in Somdeva's famous book *Kathasaritasagara (KATHA –SARITA –SAGARA)*, that is the Ocean of Stories. And I am going to perform the same role of a narrator in telling the story of Rishi Ashta-vakra.

As aforementioned, the story of Ashtavakra, appertaining his life and deeds, prominently appears in Valmiki's *Ramayana*, in the *Mahabharata*, in the *Ashtavakra Gita*, as also in Bhavabhuti's play *Uttararamacharita (UTTAR-RAMA-CHARITA)*. As per the *Mahabharata* story, Ashtavakra, born in a Brahman family, was the son of Kahoda. Kahoda was a disciple of Uddalaka. He studied in Uddalaka's *Gurukul* (school). Since he was a brilliant scholar, well-versed in the Vedas and the scriptures, his preceptor, Uddalaka, appointed him as a teacher in his school, after he finished his studies. Soon

Uddalaka married him to his daughter, Sujata. Both Kahoda and Sujata lived in the hermitage.

## ACT: ONE

## SCENE: 1

Gunadhya: Sage Uddalaka was famous for his learning and deep knowledge of scriptures. And so was Kahoda. Both taught the students in the hermitage together. In due course of time, Sujata became pregnant. She invariably followed a daily routine of sitting with her father and husband while they taught the pupils. So, the child in her womb attained mastery over the *Vedas* and other scriptures by listening to his maternal grand-father expound them. Notwithstanding the fact that Kahoda was also a great scholar, he suffered from a serious flaw of committing grammatical and other errors while reciting the scriptures. One day something extraordinary happened. The still-to-be-born child could not tolerate the errors his father made.

Ashtavakra (*Yet to be born*): Father! You are making grave errors while reciting the *shlokas* (verses). Today, you have made eight errors. And if you impart erroneous education to your students, their learning will become fallacious and flawed.

Kahoda: You are still in your mother's womb. How dare you point out the errors in my recitation! You have committed a grave sacrilege, and have thus humiliated me in the presence of my students.

Ashtavakra (still to be born): Father! I did not mean to humiliate you. My only intention was that your pupils should not learn wrong intonation and incantation.

Kahoda: You insolent, presumptuous and conceited fool! Since you have insulted me, I will punish you for your affront. Since you have a crooked mind, you will be born crooked with eight bends in your body.

## SCENE: 2

Kahoda and Sujata were poor; they could hardly make both ends meet. Their income was meager. One day Sujata got the news that Janaka, king of Mithila, had arranged a gathering of learned Brahmans for a *shastraarth* (competition among the learned and wise). It was also given out that all the Brahmans participating in the contest will be handsomely rewarded by the king. In fact, a learned scholar, named Vandin, had challenged the Brahmans, kings and princes, present in the court of Janaka, for a debate on the meaning and interpretation of scriptures.

Vandin: King! I challenge all the learned persons present in your court. Is there anyone in your kingdom who would defeat me in *shastraarth*? However, there is one stipulation. The Brahman who is defeated in the contest, will be drowned in the river.

Gunadhya: Everyone who accepted the challenge was defeated and drowned in the water. Kahoda who presumed himself to be a learned Barahman, was also vanquished. In the *Shastraarth* competion, he committed the same errors which his unborn child had pointed out. Resultantly, he lost the debate, and was drowned in the river.

A few months after Kahoda's catastrophe,

Ashtavakra was born. His mother did not tell him as to what had happened to his father. He believed that Uddalaka, his *Nanaji* (maternal grand-father), was his father, and his *mamaji* (maternal uncle), Shvetaketu, was his brother. One day, Ashtavakra, was sitting in the lap of Uddalaka.

Shvetaketu: Ashtavakra! Why are you sitting in the lap of my father?

Ashtavakra: He is my father too.

Shvetaketu: No, he is not your father. Nor am I your brother.

Ashtavakra: Then who is my father?

Shvetaketu: Go, and ask your mother.

Ashtavakra: (*Ashtavakra rushes to his mother*): Mother! Shvetaketu says that Uddalaka is not my father, nor he my brother. Then tell me mother, who is my father, and where is he?

Sujata: Dear son! Shvetaketu is correct. He is my brother, and your maternal uncle. Your father's name was Kahoda. He was a learned and wise saint. He had gone to participate in a *shastraarth* competition in the court of Janaka, the king of Mithila, where he was defeated by his rival. As per the stipulated condition of the contest, your defeated father was drowned in the water. I did not tell you your father's story, lest it should perturb and vex you.

## SCENE: 3

Gunadhya: Ashtavakra told his mother that he would go to Janaka's court, and challenge the learned Brahmans for a contest. Accompanied by Shvetketu, Ashtavakra traversed a long journey, walking with the help of a stick, and reached Mithila. Ashtavakra made his way to the palace of the king. But he was stopped at the gate by the gatekeeper. The gatekeeper asserted that inside was the assembly of learned Brahmans and kings and princes. Urchins cannot be allowed to go in.

Ashtavakra: Don't be misled by my age. I may be twelve-year old, but I am well-versed in the *Vedas* and other scriptures. Merely white hair and age do not make a man "big". One who has the knowledge of Vedas, synthesized with sharp intellect, is "big". I have come to participate in the *shastraarth* competition.

Gunadhya: The gatekeeper allowed Ashtavakra to go in. When Ashtavakra entered the king's court, everyone stared at him, and started laughing at his physical deformities. Ashtavakra looked at the conclave of supposedly learned and wise persons. For a moment, he was nonplussed and quiet. Then all of a sudden, he burst into a big horse laugh. Everyone seeing the intensity of his laughter was flabbergasted and astounded. Suddenly, everybody became quiet; there permeated a pin drop silence. King Janak was also shocked at the turn of events.

King Janaka: Child! Who are you? And why you are laughing so fervidly?

Ashtavakra: Who am I? And why am I laughing? Actually, I am pained at the people who have gathered in your court. I have been told that in your court there are the greatest of wizards who speak on subjects of high philosophy and scriptural wisdom. But I am highly disappointed. They are not learned persons. I find that in your assembly, there are only cobblers, shoe-makers.

King Janaka: What do you mean? The world knows that in my court there are persons of high learning, sages, kings and princes, who partake in the discussions on the wisdom embedded in the *Vedas* and scriptures. How can you say that they are shoe-makers?

Ashtavakra: I do not see anyone here who is learned. I only see cobblers. They only see skin like shoe-makers. They do not see the *atma* (soul). They have made their judgement on the basis of skin only. It is the business of shoe-makers to look at the skin: this skin is good, that skin is bad; this one is smooth; that one is rough. Rajan! your counselors see only the external, and not the Supreme Soul, which inhabits the body. Obviously, they are bad "soles "(souls).  And I am a mender of bad souls (soles).

## SCENE: 4

Gunadhya:  Raja Janaka and all those who were present in the assembly were greatly affected by the simple words of Ashtavakra. They felt ashamed of themselves for insulting him. The king then thought of testing the knowledge of Ashtavakra.

Janaka: What is that which has 12 parts, 24 festivals and 360 words?

Ashtavakra: May the year which has 24 holy days, six seasons, 12 months, and 360 days, protect and bless you!

Janaka: What is that which while in sleep does not close its eyes?

Ashtavakra: A fish while in sleep does not close its eyes.

Janaka: Who is that which after birth is unable to walk?

Ashtavakra: An egg even after birth cannot walk.

Janaka: Who is heartless?

Ashtavakra: A stone is heartless.

Janaka: What is that which rapidly swells and gets bigger?

Ashtavakra: It is a rivulet which speedily swells and gets bigger.

Gunadhya: The king was pleased with the enlightened knowledge and erudition of Ashtavakra. He realized that the young boy was well versed in scriptures. He, therefore, allowed him to have *shastraarth* with Vandin.

## SCENE: 5

Gunadhya: Vandin was a learned Brahman. He was the son of Varun (god of water). All those who had so far been defeated by him in the debate on scriptures, were drowned in the river. Ashtavakra's father also met the same fate. The main reason for Vandin to drown Brahmans was that his father was performing a ritual in *Varunloka*, and needed a large number of Brahmans for the said ritual. That is why Vandin drowned the defeated Brahamns in the water. Ashtavakra was aware of this fact. He challenged Vandin for a debate to teach him a lesson.

King Janaka decided to let Ashtavakra face Vandin. The debate between the two began. The condition was that they would alternatively compose impromptu / extempore verses on number one to twelve.

Vandin: One sun illuminates the whole world. Lord Indra is the only one brave god. And Yamraj (god of death) is also the only one.

Ashtavakra: Indra and Agni Dev are two gods. Narad and Mountain (that is Himavat, the personification of the Himalaya mountain, and the father of Parvati and Ganga) are two *Devarshies*. There are two Ashwin Kumars (horsemen, two Vedic deities; twin sons of the sun, or the sky. They are the harbingers of dawn, and the earliest bringer of light in the morning). A chariot has two wheels, and husband and wife are two companions.

Vandin: There are three types of births. The three *Vedas* determine the outcome of *karmas* (actions). A *yajna* is performed in three phases (time-spell). And there are three worlds (*triloki*).

Ashtavakra: There are four *ashrams* (such as Brahmachari, Grihastha, Vanaprasth, Sanyas.), four *varanas* (class or caste: *Brahman, Kshatriya, Vaisya, Sudra)*; there are four sides (East, West, North, South).

Vandin: There ae five types of *yajnas* (sacrifices); five *Indriyans* (five organs of sense: tongue, hands, feet, rectal, and genital). There are five *apsaras* (celestial nymphs); five sacred rivers.

Ashtavakra: In the south, it is a tradition to give as charity six cows; this is considered to be a noble act.

There are six seasons, and the six organs of sense, including the mind.

Vandin: There are seven types of pet animals, and seven categories of wild animals. There are seven *Rishies (sapt-rishies)*, and seven strings in a *Veena* (a stringed musical instrument).

Ashtavakra: There are eight *Vasus* (a class of deities, eight in number, chiefly Indra's attendants. They seem to have been in the *Vedic* times personifications of natural phenomena, water, moon, earth, wind, fire, dawn, light etc. According to the *Ramayana*, they were the children of Aditi).

Vandin: In the *pitri-yajna* (a type of sacrifice), nine types of ingredients are offered. And there are nine types of nature.

Ashtavakra: A child is born after ten months. And there is *daha*i, a unit of ten.

Vandin: There are eleven *Rudras* (ten vital breaths with *manas* (heart) as eleventh. scriptures postulate that the eleven R*udras* were sons of sage Kashyapa). And animals have eleven organs of sense.

Ashtavakra: There are twelve Adityas (celestial deities, sons of Aditi, representing the sun in twelve months of a year. Aditya is also one of the names of the sun). A year is of twelve months. And the *prakriti yajna* is of twelve days.

Vandin: Thirteen is a noble number. There are thirteen islands on the earth ...

Gunadhya: After having said that Vandin forgot the next line of the verse. Then he became silent.

Ashtavakra completed the thirteenth *shloka* (verse). "Agni, vayu, and the sun exist in the *yajnas* (sacrifices) for thirteen days." Thus, Vandin was defeated in the competition.

## SCENE: 6

Ashtavakra: Rajan! Vandin has lost the debate. He has been defeated in the *shastraarth*. Now is the time for us to follow the rules of the game, stipulated and practiced by Vandin himself. He should be drowned in the river, the way he has been doing with learned Brahmans all these years.

Vandin: King! I tell you the secret behind my past unethical and unholy acts. I am a son of Varun. He was performing a ritual in the *Varunloka* for which he needed learned Brahmans. That is why the Brahmans who were defeated in debate with me were drowned in the water; they thus reached the *Varunloka* to help perform the ritual. I have now realized my acts of omission and commission, for which I seek forgiveness. I will now atone for my mistake, and recall all the Brahmans from the *Varunloka*.

Gunadhya: At the instance of Vandin, all the Brahmans, including Kahoda, Ashtavakra's father, appeared in flesh and blood in the court of king Janaka.

Kahoda: I am pleased with you my son. I am meeting you after a very long time. Therefore, in you I discern my benediction. I feel extremely sad for cursing you while you were still in your mother's womb. I now make amends for my rash action taken in anger. I advise you to take a dip in the sacred river, Samanga.

Gunadhya:  On his way back home, Ashtavakra, as suggested by his father, took a dip in river Samanga. As soon as he took bath in the river, he was cured of all deformities, and emerged out of the river, as a handsome young man.

## SCENE: 7

Gunadhya:  Raja Janaka was so much impressed by the learning and wisdom of Ashtavakra that he would visit the hermitage of the sage almost regularly, and listen to his enlightened discourse. Eventually, he made the sage his *guru* (preceptor). There were a large number of monks and pupils at the *ashram* who were imparted religious and spiritual instructions by Ashtavakra. But the regular visits by the king, along with his soldiers, perturbed them. They resented the regular religious interaction between the king and the sage. The monks spoke to each other in whispers about their feelings.

Monks: Why our guru has such a rapport with king Janaka? Why should a saint dedicated to spiritual pursuits, be so deferential and subservient to a king, only because he has pelf and power?

Gunadhya: Sage Ashtavakra knew about the feelings of resentment growing among the monks. One day, the sage, while delivering a discourse, suddenly stopped and said:

Ashtavakra: O king! Your palace is on fire. Everything is burning. The whole kingdom is in chaos.

Gunadhya: But the king remained unperturbed.

However, there was panic among soldiers and other menials who had accompanied the king. He snubbed all of them, and ordered them to get away, and not pester him. However, on another day, when the sage was addressing the gathering, a helper came running.

Helper: Sire! The monkeys have taken the clothes off the clothes-line, and ran away with the "garments" of the monks.

Gunadhya: All the monks immediately got up and ran to save their clothes. But when they reached the spot, they saw no monkeys, and their lion-cloths were hanging and drying up on the clothes-line. They realized what had happened. They hung their heads in shame.

Ashtavakra: Look at these monks! They are mendicants. They have nothing except their lion cloths. They have no wife, no children, no palace. And yet they are so possessive about their lion cloths. But without paying heed to what I was saying, they ran out to save those worthless pieces of cloth. Monks! What has happened to your renunciation, so often acclaimed and professed by all of you? Look at Raja Janaka! He is a king, has a palace, wife and children, common populace to save and protect. But he did not bother, when told that his palace was on fire. He remained steadfast in listening to the religious discourse. He is a true personification of renunciation. He believes that "renunciation, not of action, but renunciation in action." What is important is not social relevance, but what is of spiritual relevance. And that is the difference between Raja Janaka and all of you.

# EPILOGUE

Ashtavakra was one of the greatest seers of India who ushered in a huge spiritual movement in his time. The philosophy of "Advaita" (non-dualism) propounded by him has been explicated in detail in *Ashtavakra Gita* (which means Song of Ashtavakra). It examines the metaphysical nature of existence and the meaning of the individual freedom. In his thesis the sage postulates that there is only one Supreme Reality, and that the entire universe is one and interconnected. The self, that is *Atman*, is part of that Supreme Reality. The *Ashtavakra Gita* is a classical *Advaita Vedanta* scripture, that is a sort of dissertation on *Advaita* philosophy. It was perhaps written after the *Bhagwat Gita*. What Lord Krishna in the *Gita* calls *loksamgraha*, that is the interconnectedness of society, qua the entire universe: the same thesis is accentuated in the *Ashtavakra Gita*, which is in the form of a dialogue between sage Ashtavakra, and Raja Janaka.

In the *Vana Parva* of the *Mahabharata*, the legend of Ashtavakra is described in detail. When the Pandavas are exiled for twelve years, one day they arrive at the hermitage of sage Lomasa, who narrates the story of Ashtavakra. He describes Ashtavakra's wisdom in the following verse:

*A grey head does not make an elder,*
*Not by years, not by grey hairs, not by riches*
*nor by relations did the seers make the law,*
*He who is great to us, is one who has learning.*

*****

# 7.RISHI GAUTAMA: THE LEGEND OF A BENEVOLENT SAGE AND AHALYA

## DRAMATIS PERSONAE

GUNADHYA: The narrator

GAUTAMA: A renowned sage

AHALYA: *Rishi* Gautama's wife; a celestial woman.

LORD BRAHMA: The God of Creation

LORD SHIVA: The Supreme God

GANESHA: A benign Deity; son of Lord Shiva

VARUN: god of Water / Ocean

INDRA: Chief of demigods

NARAD: Devarshi

VISHWAMITRA: A renowned sage

MOON: The moon god

LORD RAMA: The supreme God

SAGES AND THEIR WIVES: Rivals of *Rishi* Gautama

Goddess Ganga

Citizens

## RISHI GAUTAMA: THE LEGEND OF A BENEVOLENT SAGE AND AHALYA

## PROLOGUE

Notwithstanding performing *tapasya* (penance) for years and years, the seers of India never forgot their duties towards the mankind. By and large, they were highly benevolent and philanthropic sans any rancor, ill-will and jealousy. They were as much absorbed and saturated in their religion and spiritual obligations as in their temporal responsibilities and commitments. So much so that some of the sages even swallowed insults and humiliations without any retaliation, despite the fact that they were capable of and had the yogic and spiritual powers to hit hard on their tormentors. The mission of their life was to do good to all that exists on the earth.

Take for example *Rishi* Vishwamitra who gave to the world the famous *Gayatri Mantra*. And Rishi Markandeya blessed the world with the *Maha Mritunjaya Mantra*. Both these mantras are regularly recited by millions of people all over the globe, and seek calm of mind, solace and tranquility.

Another sage in the line of great saints, who did good to the humanity, was *Rishi* Gautama. Once there was a severe drought. The common people suffered due to paucity of rains. The famine devastated the forests, and green vegetation. *Rishi* Gautama propitiated Varun Dev (god of water / Ocean) to provide an incessant supply of water in a pond (now famous as *Gautama Kund*). The perennial pond not only fulfilled the need of drinking water of the forest-dwellers and animals, but its water was also used for irrigation.

Further, *Rishi* Gautama contributed several verses in the first Mandala of the *Rig Veda*. He also wrote a famous treatise called *Gautama Dharma Sutra*, that became famous as *Nyaya Shastra* (a book on Logic and process of reasoning) to guide the affairs of the world, qua the society at large.

## CURTAIN RAISER

My name is Gunadhya. I am a celestial being. I came to the earth in the world of mortals as a story-teller. I was the narrator of tales in Somdeva's famous book *Katha-sarita-sagara (KATHA-SARITA-SAGARA)*, that is the Ocean of Stories. And I am going to perform the same role of a narrator in telling the story of Rishi Gautama and his celestial wife, Ahalya.

*Rishi* Gautama, son of Rahugana, is one among the seven great sages (*Sapt-rishis*). He was married to Ahalya, a celestial woman, and had two sons, Vamdeva and Nodhas and a daughter named Anjani, mother of Lord Hanuman. Vamdeva has been a renowned sage. *Rishi* Gautama used to travel all over the world with the intention of helping people in distress. The *Narad Purana* describes the story of a 12-year famine. But owing to the spiritual virtues Gautama had acquired, he mitigated the sufferings of the residents of his hermitage, and did not let them experience the shortage of food and water. He even fed and helped other saints and ameliorated their lot. He turned out to be a great host. Whosoever came to his *ashram* for sustenance, he welcomed him with open arms and offered hospitality.

He led a pious life. However, there is one blemish in his life. He cursed his wife, Ahalya, for committing adultery. Later, he repented of his rash action, and made amends for his misapprehension. There is no gainsaying the fact that sage Gautama's curse, eventually turned to be a boon for Ahalya, as it shaped the course of scriptural history.

## ACT: ONE

## SCENE: 1

Gunadhya: Ahalya was an extremely beautiful girl. According to the *Ramayana*, she was the first woman created by Lord Brahma (Lord of Creation). In fact, she was mind-born daughter of Lord of Creation. Despite being charming and alluring, she was the paragon of virtues. Demigods vied with each other to woo her hand in marriage. Even the sages and saints aspired to marry her. But Lord Brahma thought to marry her to a person, who was intelligent, well-versed in the *Vedas* and scriptures and who had all the virtuous attributes and free from any blemish; who was a personification of purity, ethics, righteousness and respectability. So, Lord Brahma devised a unique plan.

Brahma: *Devas* and sages! I have decided to hold a competition to select a suitable person for the marriage of Ahalya. She will be married to a person who swiftly circumambulates the earth, and comes first in the race.

Gunadhya: All the demigods and saints moved apace to traverse around the earth. But *Rishi* Gautama did not participate in the race. He saw Kamdhenu, the divine cow, delivering a calf. Half of the calf was inside the womb of his mother, and half outside. He attended to the mother-cow to deliver the baby-cow safely. Intelligent and learned as he was, he circumambulated around the mother-Kamdhenu, regarding it with the feelings of mother-earth.

In the meantime, Lord Indra, with the help of his spiritual powers, quickly traveled around the earth, and supposedly came first in the race.

Lord Indra: Brahamdev! I have circumambulated the earth first of all. So, I have won the competition. Please consider my claim for marriage with your daughter.

Narad: Brahamdev! I want to intervene here. It is sage Gautama, not Indra, who has come first in the competition. Find out the details from *Rishi* Gautama himself.

Gautama: Respected Sire! I did not join the race to take a round of the earth. I helped Kamdhenu deliver a baby-calf. The mother-cow and her calf evoked socio-spiritual fervor and sentiments in me, making me feel that they were the representatives of the earth. So, I moved around the mother-cow; and as the scriptures postulate, it can be presumed and believed that I have taken a round of the earth, and have come first in the race.

Brahma: *Rishi* Gautama! I see your sagacity, your innate wisdom. Obviously, you know the true meaning of *dharma*. The cow which has given birth to a calf, is equal to the earth, and to do its *parikarma* (circumambulation), is like doing the *parikarma* of the earth. I am extremely pleased with your patience, and knowledge of the scriptures. Therefore, you very well deserve to marry Ahalya. I allow you and Ahalya, to live at Brahamgiri (Braham parvat / mountain), the utmost pious place, where the wishes of one and all are fulfilled.

## SCENE: 2

Gunadhya: Brahamgiri, or Braham-parvat (*parvat* means mountain), where sage Gautama and his wife, Ahalya, lived, was a holy place. There they performed *tapasya* (penance). While they were absorbed in mediation and austerities, the forest-and-mountain-dwellers around their *ashram,* faced a severe drought. It did not rain for a very long time. There was paucity of food and water. Men and animals died of hunger and thirst. Nature was also impacted by the famine; trees and plants parched and withered. In the jungles, somehow, saints kept themselves immersed in penance and passed their time. But the life for the common citizens was arduous and grim. They, then, thought of approaching sage Gautama to seek his help.

Citizens: Reverend *Rishi*! We are passing through a very difficult and trying time. Owing to drought, food and water have become scarce. People are starving. The life has become a hell. We see in you our only hope. You can save us from this calamity.

Gautama:  Don't lose patience! Have faith in Lord Shiva! He will ameliorate our lot; times will change for the better. Meanwhile, all of you can have food and water at my *ashram*. I feed a large number of *ashram*-dwellers and other saints. You too can avail of the hospitality of the hermitage.

Gunadhya: The denizens expressed their gratitude to the sage and expressed their desire to find some permanent solution to the problem. In order to help and save the populace, *Rishi* Gautama did *tapasya* to please Varun Dev, god of water; for it was he who could bring the rains to end the drought. Pleased with sage Gautama, who persuaded by his characteristic virtues of compassion and benevolence for the humanity, did tapasya to propitiate Varun. At last god of water manifested himself to him.

Varun: Sage! I am pleased with your penance, which you undertook not for yourself but for the people at large. Please ask for the boon.

Gautama:  People are suffering due to drought. I beseech you to bring rains to the parched earth.

Varun: I cannot grant this wish. It is beyond my power to bring rains. Profit-loss, life-death, drought-rainfall, heaven-hell, etc., are in the hands of Lord Shiva. He is the Master of all that happens in the world, be it drought or rainfall. Please opt for another boon that I can grant.

Gautama:  Varun Dev! In that case, please grant us an *Akshay Jal Kund* (an ever-lasting water pond).

Varun: Rishi Gautama! Dig a pond with your own hands in the forest. I will fill it with perennial water.

Gunadhya: Rishi Gautama dug a pond as directed. Varun Dev filled it with water.

## SCENE: 3

Gunadhya: The *kund* (pond) always remained filled with water; it never dried up. Soon it became famous as "Gautama Kund." With the passage of time, it became popular as a holy place for pilgrimage. Eventually, sage Gautama and his disciples, started doing farming near the pond. The news about the water pond spread like wild fire all around. Many saints with families settled near the water reservoir. They began to use the water of the pond for their domestic and drinking purpose. Soon a whole township came up there. Then something untoward happened, which changed the course of the life of sage Gautama.

Gautama: (*One day the sage asked his disciples*). Students! Go and fetch water from the pond.

Gunadhya: When the students reached the pond, they saw the wives of the *Rishis* coming fast to the pond to fetch water.

Wives: You students of *Rishi* Gautama! Stop! We will take water first. Your turn will come after we have finished taking water from the pond.

Gunadhya: The students felt humiliated. They returned without water. They complained to Ahalya about the brazen affront meted out to them by Rishi-wives.

Ahalya: Do not get perturbed! In future I will go myself to fetch water.

Gunadhya: Ahalya herself started going to the water pond. The wives of the saints got annoyed at the audacity of Ahalya. They regularly quarreled with her, even harassed and harried her. But Ahalya never reacted. She would take water from the pond and return home. But the wives of the saints would not relent. They complained to their husbands, and fed them with fake stories. At first the saints did not listen to their complaints. But the women continued to provoke them day in and day out. Eventually, they were taken in by the propaganda of their wives. The felt that both sage Gautama and his wife Ahalya were wicked.

Swayed by the falsehood of their wives, the *Rishis* confabulated together, and arrived at the conclusion that Gautama and Ahalya were errant-duo, and needed to be taught a lesson. They devised a plan to invoke Lord Ganesha, and seek his help.

Ganesha: Saints! Why have you invoked me? What do you want from me?

*Rishis*: Both sage Gautama and his wife, Ahalya, have been troubling us, and pestering and insulting our wives. We urge upon you to punish both of them and banish them from their hermitage.

Ganesh: Listen saints! Your desire is not pious. It smacks of rancor. I am not inclined to fulfill it. And if you insist on it, then you would invite destruction for yourself.

*Rishis*: Benign Lord! Sage Gautama and his wife insulted and humiliated us without any justifiable reason. We demand that you should punish them.

Ganesha: Sage Gautama has the blessings of Lord Shiva. As such no harm can come to him.

Gunadhya: Lord Ganesh realized that the demand of the *Rishis* was unjust and unfair. Yet he decided to grant it. For he felt that the *Rishis* and their wives warranted to be penalized for their dereliction. Then

Lord Ganesha disappeared.

## SCENE: 4

Gunadhya: Sage Gautama did not know that the *Rishis* were inimical to him and had hatched a conspiracy against him. He had cultivated some fields and sowed paddy and other grains in them. His daily routine was to go to the fields with his students and tend them. One day, Lord Ganesha took the form of a sick cow, and began to eat the standing crops. The sage saw the cow damaging the crop. He tried to drive it away with a blade of grass. But as ill luck would have it, he erroneously hit the cow with that blade of grass. The cow fell down and died.

The *Rishi* who was waiting for a ruse to harm Gautama and his wife, found an opportunity to accomplish their evil design. They shouted in unison.

Rishis: Look! What has Gautama done? He has killed a cow. The killing of a cow is a grave sin; it will bring terrible calamity. Banish him along with his wife from this hermitage.

Gunadhya: The *Rishis* abused Gautama and his wife, pelted stones at them, and drove them away. Gautama abandoned the hermitage, and set another *ashram* some distance away. The *Rishis* completely disassociated themselves from Gautama and Ahalya, and socially boycotted them.

Gautama: I am a sinner. I am guilty of cow-killing. Till I expiate of my guilt, I would not touch anyone; I would refrain from performing any sacrifice or other religious ceremonies. (*After a few days sage*

*Gautama approached the Rishis)*. Sages! I want to free myself from the sin I committed. I seek your advice and guidance to atone for my guilt.

Rishis: Gautama! We have full sympathy with you. Your wife and disciples disrespected and denigrated our wives. You will have to bear the consequence of this unacceptable behavior. Nevertheless, in order to diminish your torments, we tell you a solution. First, travel around the earth. After that pray very hard for a month. And then circumambulate Brahamgiri mountain a hundred times. And finally bring Ganga at this place and bathe in it. This will complete your atonement and you would become free from the sin of cow-killing.

## **SCENE: 5**

Gunadhya: As proposed by the Rishis, Gautama and his wife, Ahalya, performed all the tasks. After that they immersed themselves in severe *tapasya* to propitiate Lord Shiva. At last, Lord Shiva manifested himself to them.

Lord Shiva: Gautama! I am pleased with your penance. Please ask for the boon.

Gautama: Mahadev! Please free me from the sin of cow-killing.

Lord Shiva: Sage! You have been hoodwinked by the *Rishis*. You have committed no sin. You have suffered for no fault of yours. All those who caused pain to you will be penalized. For any person who harasses and torments my devotee, will never be happy.

Gautama: I do not blame the *Rishis* for my

sufferings. In fact, they have done me a good. If they had not indulged in this kind of conduct, I would not have got the blessings of your manifestation.

Lord Shiva: I am happy with your devotion and benevolent nature. Demand! What do you want?

Gautama: Please grant me the boon of the presence of goddess Ganga in my hermitage.

Gunadhya: Lord Shiva put down goddess Ganga from his matted hair, and gave her to sage Gautama.

Lord Shiva: O Devi Ganga! Think *Rishi* Gautama to be your *sevak* (servant). And cleanse him from all sins.

Goddess Ganga: I will always be present here near sage Gautama's *ashram.* But there is one stipulation; that both Lord Shiva and Devi Parvati be always present in the hermitage.

Lord Shiva: *Tathastu.* (Be it so).

Gautama: Mahadev! I know that the *Rishis* and their wives acted wickedly. But they should be pardoned for their delinquency. However, in order to expiate for their guilt, they should perform penance by circling around Braham-parvat hundred-and-one times.

Rishis: *Rishi* Gautama! Please pardon us! We seek your forgiveness for our wicked deeds.

Gunadhyaa: Goddess Ganga started flowing in the form of a river, and became famous by the name of "Gautamai." That is "Gautamai Ganga."Both Lord Shiva and Devi Parvati stayed put there. Lord Shiva established "Trymbakeshwar," (that is the three-eyed God) the eighth *Jyotirlinga* at that place. The river Ganga which flowed from there came to be known as Godavri. Ganga, Gautamai Ganga, and Godavri, are the same.

## SCENE: 6

Gunadhya: Lord Indra was infatuated by the beauty of Ahalya. Despite having failed to marry her, he nurtured an evil desire to seduce her. *Rishi* Gautama lived in his *ashram* with his wife peacefully. He was ignorant of the evil intentions of Indra. He followed his daily routine of getting up early in the morning much before goddess Aurora appeared in the firmament. He would go to river Ganga in the wee hours for the morning ablutions. Indra knew about the sage's morning routine. One day he decided to put his evil design into practice.

Indra: Chandra Dev (The Moon god)! I entrust an errand to you. Please assume the form of a cock and crow at midnight much before sage Gautama usually wakes up for his morning ablutions.

Moon: Lord Indra! I am sorry I cannot do that. I cannot be a party to your wickedness. When sage Gautama comes to know of this, he will punish me with a curse.

Indra: If you don't obey me, I will penalize you. I am your king. You have to obey my order.

Gunadhya: Moon disappeared from the sky, creating an impression that it was going to be morning. Then he assumed the form of a cock and crowed. Hearing the crowing of the cock, sage Gautama woke up as usual. And so also Ahalya. He left his cottage and walked towards river Ganga for morning chores and a holy bath.

Finding Ahalya alone in the cottage, Indra assumed the form of Rishi Gautama, and in that disguise, he entered the cottage.

Ahalya: Swami! How is it that you have returned so soon!

Indra: On way to the Ganga, I was suddenly overtaken by a romantic mood. So, I decided to return midway.

Gunadhya: Indra's ruse worked. He outraged the chastity of Ahalya. When sage Gautama reached river Ganga, and readied himself for a holy dip, goddess Ganga appeared:

Goddess Ganga: Sage! How is it that instead of coming at 4 am, you have come today at midnight at 2 am to disturb me?

Gautama: I woke up as usual when the cock crowed.

Goddess Ganga: You have been tricked.

Gunadhya: Saying this Devi Ganga disappeared. Gautama felt that he might have committed an error of judgement. So, he returned to his cottage without taking a bath. When he reached home, he saw a person who resembled him in his appearance. With his yogic power he visualized that the person in front of him was Indra, assuming his appearance. He could also perceive to his dismay the grave sin Indra had committed.

Gautama:  Indra! You have misled a chaste woman into an outrageous act. I curse you with impotency, with one thousand genitalia (*sahasra yonis*)

Gunadhya: When Ahalya heard the commotion, she came out running. When she saw two men having similar appearance of her husband, she visualized as to what had happened.

Ahalya: Alas! I have been tricked.

Gautama: What is the use of repenting now? How could you not recognize him?

Ahalya: He looked exactly like you; he resembled you.

Gautama:  You are a wife of a self-realized sage. You should have looked inside you. Then you would have known the truth and escaped ignominy. You too have committed a sin. I curse you to become a stone.

Gunadhya: Ahalya instantly turned into a stone. Sage Gautama also cursed the moon to have scars.

Ahalya: Swami! I have not done anything wrong. I request you to please take the curse back.

Gautama: That is not possible.

Ahalya: Then, Swami, take pity on me, and limit the span of the curse to a specified period.

Gautama: When Lord Rama, accompanied by *Rishi* Vishwamitra, on his way to Mithila, comes to this hermitage, He will free you from this curse. Then you will assume your original celestial form and go to heaven.

## SCENE: 7

Gunadhya: The *Ramayana* has it that when Lord Rama, on his way to Mithila, came to a desolate *ashram,* he saw a stone among ruins, out of which was sprouting a *tulsi* plant. He enquired from his guru:

Lord Rama: Guru Vishwamitra! Look at this stone! A *tulsi* plant is emanating out of it. This is amazing. All around everything is in ruins. Please tell me the secret of this riddle.

Vishwamitra: Inside this stone lives the soul of a noble woman. She is an unfortunate woman, who was deceived by one man, and cursed by another. She is Ahalya, who was cursed by her own husband, *Rishi* Gautama. Ram! Everyone knows how to blame and punish a wrong-doer, but there are a few special persons who have the power to redeem the fallen. And you are that special person. It is ordained that the touch of your feet will redeem this penitent woman. So, touch that stone with your foot and redeem Ahalya from the curse.

Gunadhya: As directed by his preceptor, Lord Rama redeemed Ahalya from that curse.

Ahalya: Lord Rama! My Husband cursed me and turned me into a stone. But now I realize that that curse actually turned out to be a boon for me. Had I not been cursed; I would not have the blessings of your manifestation. I am certainly a privileged woman who is looking the incarnation of the Supreme Being face to face.

Lord Rama:  Your pain and suffering have now been turned into benediction. You have achieved *moksha* (deliverance, freedom).

# EPILOGUE

Ancient scriptures propound that the human mind has supremacy over the matter. And so assert the sages and prophets that on this earth there is nothing great but man, and in man there is nothing great but mind, for the mind is all. The powers of mind are like the rays of the sun, when concentrated and invoked, they illumine. One can see the manifestation of the powers of the human mind in the ancient seers of India. They undertook arduous *tapasya* not for any temporal gain, but for the benefit of the mankind. The aim of their austerities, by and large, has been altruistic and humanitarian. *Rishi* Gautama appeased Lord Shiva and brought Gautami Ganga, qua river Godavri, for the amelioration of the conditions of the people at large. The sage used to travel all over the world with the intention of helping humanity. He had mastered the art of great *Savitri* Mantra. The *Narad Purana* describes the story of 12-year famine during which sage Gautama fed many other sages and saved them from hunger.

Another significant contribution of sage Gautama is the *Nyaya Shastra*, a unique philosophy, appertaining logic and the process of reasoning. *Nyaya* means logical analysis. Those who subscribe to this philosophy believe that the perception of valid knowledge brings *moksha* (deliverance). Gautama's teachings are also called *Gautama Sutra, or Gautama Smriti*.

However, the sage is often criticized for one blemish. He cursed his wife, and turned her into a stone. The critics aver that Ahalya was punished unnecessarily for she had not committed any fault or sin. She was tricked into a wrong act by the appearance of the trickster who had assumed the form of her husband. Perhaps Rishi Gautama acted rashly. He did not consider the pros and cons. But eventually the "pros" turned out to be more than the "cons." For the curse brought Ahalya face to face with the Supreme Lord, who, with the touch of His lotus feet, granted her *moksha*. The adversity became salubrious.

*****

# 8.RISHI ATRI AND ANASUYA, THE DIVINE MOTHER

## DRAMATIS PERSONAE

GUNADHYA: The narrator

ATRI: A renowned sage

ANASUYA: Sage Atri's wife, a divine mother

TRINITY: Brahma, Vishnu, Mahesh

CONSORTS: Devi Saraswati, Lakshmi and Parvati, wives

of Trinity

ASWIN KUMARS: The *Vedic* Deities

MANDAVYA: A sage

KAUSHIK: A citizen, a brahmin

Kaushik's wife

A prostitute

Demigods

Demons

# RISHI ATRI AND ANASUYA, THE DIVINE MOTHER

## PROLOGUE

Rishi Atri is one of the mind-born (*manas- putra*) son of Brahma, the Lord of Creation. He is one of the most popular *sapt-rishis* (seven sages). The seven sages are extolled in many places in the *Vedas,* and the *Puranas*, as also in the *Mahabharata* and the *Ramayana.* Significantly, they are regarded as the patriarchs of the *Vedic* religion. It is from these Rishis that *gotras* are derived. In fact, Hindus, by and large, are the *Rishi Santan* (the descendants of the sages). Hence the *gotra* like Bharadwaja, Kashyap, Atri, Prashar, Vats, etc. formed lineage a large number of Hindu families. There is no gainsaying the fact that the seers of the ancient India are the ancestors of the Hindus. The sages of the antiquity were entrusted with the task of passing on the knowledge, they had acquired. to humanity for the good of the people at large. They played a very important role in accumulating and dispersing all the knowledge that we have received today. They have been equated with the Seven Stars of the constellation, Ursa Major (the Great Bear, *Sapt-rishi Tarey*, that is the stars of S*apt-rishis):* and Big Dipper (the seven principal stars in the constellation of Ursa Major arranged in a form of a dipper).

As aforementioned, Atri is one of the most celebrated and distinguished *Sapt-rishis*. He is prominently mentioned in the *Rig Veda,* in other scriptures and in the classical literature. The *Fifth Mandla* of the *Rig Veda* has been named as *Atri*

*Mandla* in honor of this great seer. He was married to Anasuya, a celestial woman, and one of the seven chaste women (*pativrata*); she was in fact an epitome of virtues. Sage Atri had three sons, Soma (Moon), Datta-treya and Durvasa; all the three were born with the blessings of the *Trinity*, Brahma, Vishnu, Mahesh respectively.

## CURTAIN RAISER

My name is Gunadhya. I am a celestial being. I came to the earth in the world of mortals as a story-teller. I was the narrator of tales in Somdeva's *Katha-sarita-sagara (KATHA–SARITA –SAGARA)*, that is the Ocean of Stories. And I am going to perform the same role of a narrator in telling the story of *Rishi* Atri and his wife, Anasuya, the divine mother.

There are many wondrous legends connected with sage Atri. One of them is the rescuing of the sun from the demon Rahu. Demon Rahu had eclipsed the sun, thereby creating darkness in all the three worlds (*Triloki*). This created panic. The demigods, at the instance of Lord Brahma, approached *Rishi* Atri who rescued the sun from the clutches of Rahu. There is yet another story. Atri was once captured by *rakshas* (demons). They threw him into a dungeon and wanted to burn him alive. But he was rescued by Aswin Kumars, the *Vedic* deities.

## ACT: ONE

## SCENE: 1

Gunadhya: There appears two verses in the *Rig*

*Veda*, which describe how sage Atri liberated the sun, who was seized by demon Rahu. "When Svarbhanu (a synonym for Rahu) of the *Asur* race pierced thee, O sun, with darkness, all worlds appear like a man who is bewildered in a region with which he is not familiar." And again "when Indra, thou didst sweep away the magical wiles of Svarbhanu which were operating beneath the sky, Atri discovered (rather recovered), the sun which had been hidden by the hostile darkness."

Demigods: Sage Atri! Svarbhanu, who fought on behalf of the *rakshas* (demons), has completely covered the sun, and blocked the light. We, the gods, have collectively resolved to request you to defeat the demon, and rescue the sun, so that the world gets the light again. We know you have the powers of the prayers and of the mantras to do so.

Atri: It is my bounden duty to serve and please the demigods. I condemn the act of demon Rahu to mask the sun, cloaking the world in darkness. With the powers I have acquired through many years of penance, I will wrest the sun out of the hands of Rahu, and restore the light.

## SCENE: 2

Gunadhya: Atri freed the sun from the clutches of Rahu. The world, once again, shimmered in the light. The demigods were extremely pleased. Nevertheless, there is another wondrous happening which again manifests the yogic power of *Rishi* Atri. Since the demons were inimical to sage Atri, they caught him one day, and threw him into a pit. They intended to scorch him in fire, when Aswin Kumars came to his rescue. Aswin Kumars, twin sons of the sun or the sky, are two *Vedic* deities. They literally mean "horsemen." are ever young and handsome, agile, swift, possessed of many forms. They are the earliest bringers of light in the morning sky. As personifications of the morning twilight, they are said to be children of the sun by a nymph who concealed herself in the form of a mare; hence she was called Aswin, and her sons Aswin Kumars. In Sanskrit "Aswa, or Ashwa "means a horse.

Demons: Atri has been our enemy. He has been a prominent priestly leader of the tribe antagonistic to us. We are happy that he has been caught. Throw him into a dungeon and burn him alive.

Gunadhya: When Atri was captured, he was in a meditative trance. In that state of mind, he could not know as to what had happened to him. When he felt the heat of the fire, he stirred to animation, and immediately remembered Aswins.

Aswin Kumars: *Rishi* Atri has remembered us. He seems to be in peril. We visualize that he is in *smadhi* (meditative trance). Demons are trying to scorch him to death. Let us help him out and save his life.

Gunadhya: Aswins rescued sage Atri from the stranglehold of *Asuras* (demons). This legend appears in the *First Mandala* of the *Rig Veda*.

Atri: Aswin Kumars! I am beholden to you for saving my life. You appeared at the right time to liberate me from the captivity of the *Asuras*, who were ill-disposed towards me.

Aswin Kumars: *Rishi* Atri! You have been a benevolent saint. You rescued the sun from the grip of demon Rahu, and thus restored the light. Since you have been doing good to the mankind in general, and your tribe in particular, we grant you the boon of eternal youth.

Gunadhya: The legend of Aswin Kumars granting eternal youth to Atri, and the severe *tapasya* performed by him, appears in the *Tenth Mandala* of the *Rig Veda*.

## SCENE: 3

Gunadhya: Anasuya was married to sage Atri. She was a pious woman, practicing austerities. She is described as having miraculous powers. As implied in her name, Anasuya literally means "free from any envy or jealousy." Anasuya is composed of two Sanskrit words – 'Nah,' and 'Asuya.' 'Nah,' a negative prefix, meaning absence, while 'Asuya,' means jealousy. There is an interesting story appertaining Anasuya. A Brahmin, named Kaushik, used to visit a prostitute, notwithstanding having a devoted wife at home. Owing to his wayward and recalcitrant acts and behavior, he soon became infected with a serious disease.

Prostitute: Kaushik! Since you suffer from contagious disease, I warn you not to come here again. Please return to your wife who still cares for you.

Kaushik: But I am in love with you. I long for your company and affection.

Prostitute: Nothing doing. You will not come here again.

Gunadhya: But Kaushik was almost mad for the harlot's love. One day, he coerced his wife, a caressing, caring and devoted woman, to take him to the prostitute. In that town there lived a sage, named Mandavya. He had been impaled for committing a crime, and was lying in spikes in the forest. While on his way to meet the whore, Kaushik led by his wife, walked through the forest in the night. Sage Mandavya was sleeping. Kaushik did not see him in the darkness of the night. And he unknowingly tripped on the sage. The sage got annoyed, and cursed him.

Mandavya: You fool! Your infatuation for a whore has made you blind that you could not see a man lying in your way, and have trampled upon him. I curse you that you will die as soon as the sun rises tomorrow morning.

Kaushik's Wife: Since I am a *pativrata* (devoted wife), I will restrain the sun from rising tomorrow. Let there be darkness all over the universe.

Demigods: (*Alarmed by the uncanny happening, the gods went post-haste to Lord Brahma, and sought his intervention*). Brahamdev! A *pativrata* woman, devoted to her husband, has inhibited the sun from rising tomorrow morning. This will create havoc in the three worlds.

Brahamdev: Only Anasuya, a *pativrata*, can convince another *pativrata* to undo the curse. You are advised to approach Anasuya. She will persuade Kaushik's wife to allow the sun to appear in the firmament as usual tomorrow morning.

Gunadhya: Demigods approach Anasuya in her *ashram*, and tell her the whole story. She assures the gods that she will convince Kaushik's wife to withdraw her curse.

Anasuya: Sister! Allow the sun to rise! Your husband is not at fault. He stumbled over the saint unknowingly. Please undo the curse. I assure you to bring your husband back to life after the sage's curse has run its course.

Brahma: (*The Lord of Creation manifests himself to Anasuya*). Anasuya! I am pleased with you. You have the blessings of the Trinity.

## SCENE: 4

Gunadhya: Anasuya and her husband, Atri, lived in a small hermitage, situated at Chitrakut. She was a pious woman. Like her husband, she practiced austerities, and had acquired supernatural powers. She was devoted and loyal to her husband, and could not be misled by the enticements of Gods and demigods. She is rightly considered as one of the famous *pativratas* of the ancient India. Devi Saraswati, Devi Lakshmi and Devi Parvati, the consorts of Brahma, Vishnu, Mahesh, respectively, wanted to learn the merits of *pativrata dharma* (purity, chastity) from Anasuya.

Consorts: Lords! We three, Saraswati, Lakshmi and Parvati, have heard that Anasuya, wife of *Rishi* Atri, is a paragon of chastity and a paradigm of devotion to her husband. We seek your permission to go to her in human form to learn the quality and merit of *pativrata dharma* from her.

Trinity: Devis! First, let us go there to appraise her purity and devotion. After we have tested her loyalty to her husband, we will take further decision whether you should go there or not.

Gunadhya: Brahma, Vishnu and Mahesh, disguised

themselves as hermits, knocked at the gate of the hermitage, and vociferously shouted "Bhikshan dehi" (give us alms).

Anasuya: (*Coming out at the gate of the ashram, and looking at the hermits with motherly affection*) Hermits! Wait a while. I will give you alms. Let me go in and bring some food for you.

Trinity: Devi! We don't accept alms like that. You have to give us alms totally naked sans clothes.

Gunadhya: (*Hearing this, Anasuya was flabbergasted*). But with the yogic powers, she could visualize as to who they were. She transformed them into new-born babies, removed her clothes, and started breast-feeding them with motherly love. Thus, she kept her social obligation of giving alms to the hermits, as well as protected her chastity. Meanwhile, the wives of the three principal Gods (Trinity) waited for the return of their husbands. But when they did not turn up for long, together they decided to travel to Anasuya's cottage to take stock of the situation.

Consorts: Look! There they are, transformed into small babies. We must beseech Devi Anasuya to pardon our husbands, and restore them to their original forms.

Gunadhya: The consorts of the Trinity, then, revealed their identities to Anasuya, and sought her forgiveness. Anasuya restored the trinity to their original state.

Trinity: Devi Anasuya! We are pleased with your chastity and your devotion towards your husband. Please ask for the boon. What do you want?

Anasuya: I desire that I should breast-feed you three as my sons.

Trinity: *Tathastu* (Be it so). We, the three Gods, grant you this wish.

Gunadhya: With the passage of time, there were born three sons, namely Soma, Datta-treya, and Duirvasa. Soma (Moon), Datta-treya, and Durvasa, were the sons of Brahma, Vishnu and Shiva, respectively.

## SCENE: 5

Gunadhya: There appears an extremely important story in the *Ramayana*, Lord Rama, during the period of exile, had visited the hermitage of *Rishi* Atri at Chitrakut. It was here that *sati* Anasuya explained to another *sati*, Devi Sita, consort of Lord Rama, about the grandeur and importance of *satitva* (unflinching devotion to husband). It is an extremely significant episode.

Anasuya: Devi Sita! Every married woman should strictly observe the *pativrata dharma* (loyalty to her husband*)* *Satitva* is the bulwark of a chaste and devoted wife. Let me deliver a discourse on this subject to make you understand the merits of *pativrata dharma.*

Gunadhya: Devi Sita listened to the discourse very attentively. At the same time Anasuya was extremely affectionate and kind to her.

Anasuya: Devi Sita! Besides observing *satitva*, a woman should always appear before her husband embellished in ornaments and tempting clothes. I, therefore, give you these divine clothes and ornaments. And this is an unction which will keep you look young and beautiful always.

Gunadhya:   After having heard the discourse on *satitva*, Sita touched the feet of Anasuya, the celestial mother. Then she departed with the divine gifts Anasuya had given to her.

## EPILOGUE

Why was sage Atri captured by demons and thrown into a pit to be scorched. The reasons were socio-historical. The *Vedic* Aryan tribes were ambitious and war-like. From their homes in the tribal regions, these adventurers set out on a mission of conquest and colonization towards the south-east. This, however, was not an easy task. On their onward march, these people who were really the ancestors of the Vedic Indians, had to encounter serious opposition from several antagonistic tribes. Atri seems to have been one of the Aryan colonizers. As such he must have been arrested and persecuted by the non-Aryan inhabitants of India. They threw him into a burning pit to kill him. From this disaster the Aswins seem to have saved him.

Atri must have been a popular leader and a zealous missionary. This is not only borne out by the fact that he is referred to as *pancajanya* (that is five peoples, coming under the political dominance of five states, and monarchical kingdoms). *Pancajanya* may also mean "one who acts for the welfare of five tribes."

Further, the *Vedas* and the post-*Veda* scriptures substantiate the efficacy of the prayers and the Mantras. The *Vedic* priests seem to be anxious to impress upon the people the fact that it was not merely the valor of India, or the warriors, which helped towards victory. In order to be really effective that valor had to be necessarily aided by the magic power of prayers and Mantras. It will not be wrong to point out that Atri rescued the sun by means of his prayers / Mantras. And something similar might have happened in his escape from fire when he was thrown into a dungeon by demons, and Aswins invoked to help him rescue. The prominence of this *Rishi* can be ascertained from the fact that he is one of the stars of the Great Bear.

*****

# 9.RISHI DADHICHI: A BENEVOLENT SAGE WHO DONATED HIS BONES

## DRAMATIS PERSONAE

GUNADHYA: The narrator

DADHICHI: A Renowned Seer

TVASHTA: A sage

VRITRA: A ferocious demon

INDRA: Chief of the demigods

SHUKRACHARYA: Guru of *Asuras* (demons)

THE TRINITY: Lord Brahma, Lord Vishnu, Lord Shiva

KSHUVA: A king in ancient India

A Shepherd

# RISHI DADHICHI: A BENEVOLENT SAGE WHO DONATED HIS BONES

## PROLOGUE

The sages of ancient India were highly altruistic. They were humanitarian and magnanimous. They did *tapas* (penance) not for self-aggrandizement but for the benefit of all mankind, nay of all creation. Since they were human beings, sometimes they exhibited human weaknesses. However, there is no gainsaying the fact that they were, by and large, benign and bounteous. *Rishi* Dadhichi has been one such saint who willingly offered his bones to save *devas* (demigods) from being routed by *asuras* (demons). He was known, far and wide, for his supernatural powers. Yet at the same time he was acclaimed for his munificence.

According to the *Bhagavata Purana*, Dadhichi was the son of Atharvan, who is believed to be the author of the *Atharva-veda*. His mother, Chitti, was the daughter of sage Kardam. The names of Dadhichi's wife and son were Swarcha and Pippalada respectively. Both Kardam and Pippalada were respected as great seers. So, Dadhichi hailed from an illustrious family. Dadhichi's son, Pippalada, was born after the death of his parents. Since there was nobody to take care of him, he was abandoned under a pipal tree. Hence his name Pippalada. The mystical significance refers to the association of the pipal tree with initiation, or *nirvanic* attainment. It was under a pipal tree that Gautama Buddha is believed to have attained *nirvana*. Pippalada is known for creating the *Prasna Upanishad* where he answers the queries of his pupils.

## CURTAIN RAISER

My name is Gunadhya. I am a celestial being. I came to the earth in the world of mortals as a story teller. I was the narrator of tales in Somdeva's *Kathasaritasagara (KATHA-SARITA-SAGARA)*, that is the Ocean of Stories. And I am going to perform the same role of a narrator in telling the story of *Rishi* Dadhichi who sacrificed his life so that demigods could survive and defeat *asuras* (demons).

There are many fantastic tales connected with this seer. Right from his early childhood, Dadhichi was a courageous, fearless person, dedicated to the welfare of all living beings, man, birds and beasts. He was magnanimity personified, a paragon of munificence, a human being par excellence.

There is an interesting tale appertaining his boyhood, which substantiates the adage: "The child shows the man / As morning shows the day." In this tale we visualize Dadhichi, the way he would go when he becomes old, and would not depart from this path.

## ACT: ONE

## SCENE: 1

Gunadhya: Once a poisonous snake climbed a tree, and caught a chick of parrots having their nest in the hole of a tree. The parrots made a lot of noise which attracted the farmers working in the nearby fields. A young shepherd who was grazing his sheep close by, too heard the noise. All of them came running. A swarm of people collected there. But none from the crowd of onlookers dared try to free the parrot-chick from the stranglehold of the snake. Dadhichi, still in his boyhood, was playing with his friends in the close proximity of the tree. He too heard the commotion. He abandoned his play, sauntered close to the tree and saw a parrot-chick in the hold of a snake. Taking stock of the predicament of the birds as well as of the crowd of people for a moment, he immediately climbed the tree and with a stick he freed the parrot chick from the clutches of the snake. Before the snake could retaliate and bite him, he jumped down from the tree. The fall caused multiple injuries to him. But he did not care. The young shepherd could not resist his temptation to accost Dadhichi.

Shepherd: Boy! We appreciate your dare. But why did you put your life in peril for a bird?

Dadhichi: It is the duty of every man to protect a living being, be it a man or a bird. Seeing the parrot family in serious danger, I could not turn a blind eye and a deaf ear to the uncanny situation.

Shepherd: Dadhichi! Did you not fear the poisonous snake? It could have bitten you, which might have resulted in your death.

Dadhichi: Fear! What is fear? It is only a condition of mind. When you free your mind from any unforeseen danger, you become fearless, and acquire courage to fight against any horror. Nevertheless, we should be apprehensive of doing iniquitous and reprehensible acts. One who does good deeds, God protects and blesses him.

Gunadhya: Dadhichi then left the crowd ruminating over what had happened. The very sentiments of *lok raksha* (public welfare/protection) expressed by Dadhichi eventually accentuated into a strong determination when he offered his bones to gods sans any hem and haw.

## SCENE: 2

Gunadhya: In the hackneyed old times, there was a king named Kshuva, a devotee of Lord Vishnu. He was a friend of Dadhichi. One day a dispute arose between the two friends. They got into an argument which took an ugly turn,

Kshuva: Dadhichi! You are a Brahman. You did *tapasya* and acquired supernatural powers. But that does not make a Brahman superior to a King. A king arranges for the maintenance of his subjects; protects their life and honour. He is the representative of the Supreme on the earth. I am, therefore, superior to you.

Dadhichi: Kshuva! No, I do not agree with you. Brahmans are superior to *Kshatriya, Vaish and Sudra.*

Kshuva: Kings not Brahmans are superior. I, as a king, am the biggest god.

Dadhichi: Think on the matter dispassionately. And don't dare insult me. Your arguments are against the scriptures.

Gunadhya: But the king stuck to his opinion. The arguments became acrimonious and acrid. Dadhichi lost the cool of his mind. He hit the king Kshuva with the fist of his left hand on his fore-head. Kshuva too became angry. He retaliated fiercely. He cut Dadhichi with *Vajra* (Thunderbolt). Dadhichi fell flat on the ground grievously injured. At that moment of exigency, he remembered his *guru* Shukracharya.

Shukracharya: Dadhichi! With the *mritsanjivini* mantra (life-giving mantra) given to me by Lord Shiva, I will join the cut off parts of your body, and revive you to life. I, however, urge upon you to recite *Maha Mritunjaya* Mantra to propitiate Lord Shiva who will protect you always.

Gunadhya: After reviving Dadhichi to health, Shukracharya departed. Unable to bear the insult and the humiliation Dadhichi suffered at the hands of his friend, now turned foe, he went to the mountains, and engrossed in *tapasya* (penance). At last Lord Shiva manifested Himself to him.

Lord Shiva: Dadhichi! I am pleased with your penance. Ask for the boon.

Dadhichi: Mahadev! Kindly grant me three boons. First, my bones should become *vajra* (as hard as a diamond); second, I could never be killed; and third, I should never be humiliated.

Lord Shiva: *Tathastu*! Be it so.

Gunadhya: Having equipped himself with the three boons, Dadhichi returned to king Kshuva to take revenge. The sage hit the king on his head with his leg. The king, in anger, hit the sage with *vajra*. But it did not cause any harm to the sage. The *vajra* was rendered ineffective, thanks to the boon of Lord Shiva. Kshuva, being a staunch devotee of Lord Vishnu, approached Him for help.

Kshuva: Lord! There is a Brahman, named Dadhichi. Earlier he was my friend. These days, owing to severe *tapasya*, Lord Shiva has made him all powerful. Recently, he came to my court, and hit me with his left leg on my head and arrogantly said:

"I am not afraid of anybody." Please take pity on me and avenge my insult and punish the delinquent sage.

Lord Vishnu: Rajan! Brahmans have no fear. And for a devotee of Lord Shiva, there is nothing like fear, not even a bit of it. If I act against him, on your behalf, he may curse me too. Therefore, I will have to tackle him tactfully. King! I recall how I was defeated by Shiva during my participation in the *Yajna* of Daksha. Therefore, I will devise some plan to act to win him over for you. I will disguise myself as a Brahman and go to sage Dadhichi's *ashram*. After paying my adoration and veneration to the sage, I will ask for a boon for you.

Dadhichi: Brahman! I am a devotee of Lord Shiva. As such I am a *trikaldarshi* (one who can see the past, present and future). Therefore, I visualize that you are not a Brahman, but Lord Vishnu in disguise, and that you have come to demand something for your devotee, king Kshuva. Abandon this *maya* (illusion) and return to your original divine form. Tell me, what is there in your mind? What do you want?

Lord Vishnu: Sage! I have come to seek a small favour from you. Munificent as you are, I hope you will not deny me my desire.

Dadhichi: What is that?

Lord Vishnu: I want you to go to king Kshuva, and tell him: "Rajan! I am afraid of you."

Dadhichi: (*Smiling at the words of Lord Vishnu*). Owing to the blessings of Lord Shiva, I am not afraid of anybody.

Gunadhya: Annoyed at the curt reply of Dadhichi, Lord Vishnu tried to persuade him coercively. Even demigods, who had accompanied Lord Vishnu, assisted him in the duress. Soon, there ensued a brawl, a clash. Dadhichi defeated all of them. The demigods ran away from there. But Lord Vishnu stayed put.

In the meantime, king Kshuva arrived at the hermitage of sage Dadhichi. He stopped Lord Vishnu and others from escalating the dispute.

Kshuva: Sage! I know you are a devotee of Lord Shiva. You have Mahadev's blessings. No harm can come to you. I pay my obeisance to you. Please be pleased with me. And be kind to me.

Lord Vishnu: As you have desired, I abandon my disguise, and return to my original divine form.

Dadhichi: I revere you Lord Vishnu. Your presence and the supplication of your devotee, king Kshuva, have made me compassionate. I now reconcile to him. Rajan! I reiterate that Brahmans are superior to and more powerful than kings.

Gunadhya: After that Dadhichi returned to his ashram, and king Kshuva went back to his kingdom.

## SCENE: 3

Gunadhya: Once upon a time, Indra was sitting on his throne, and other gods were seated around him. Gandharvas were singing, and *apsaras* (celestial dancers) were dancing. Suddenly, Brihaspati, the *guru* of the *devas* (demigods) came to the Assembly. But Indra was so engrossed in enjoying the singing and dancing that he neglected to stand up and honour

Brihaspati. The preceptor of demigods felt insulted, and left the Assembly in anger. Indra soon realized his mistake. He decided to find out his *guru* and beg his forgiveness. But Brihaspati was nowhere to be found. Using his powers of *maya*, he had simply vanished.

*Asuras* got to know that the demigods were now without a preceptor. They thought that this was an opportune moment to attack the *devas*. After seeking permission of Shukracharya, the *guru* of *asuras* (demons), they attacked the gods, and drove them out of heaven. The demigods went running to Lord Brahma.

Lord Brahma: Indra! You are responsible for your predicament. All this has happened because you humiliated your *guru*. Since you have no *guru*, you have become weak. Go and pray to sage Vishvarupa, the son of Tvashta. He will find a way out.

Gunadhya: Tvashta had married Rachana who was a *daitya* (demon) woman, and it was inconceivable that he would help the demigods in their fight against demons. But when the demigods prayed to Vishvarupa, he could not refuse. He became the priest of gods, and acting on his advice, *devas* defeated the *asuras*.

Indra was never sure of Vishvarupa. He was after all related to the demons. He might help *asuras* secretly when he got the chance. So, he killed Vishvarupa. Tvashta was furious when he came to know that Indra had killed his son, Vishvarupa. He performed a *yajna* and wished that an enemy of Indra might be born out of the flames. A terrible demon came out of the *yajna* fire. He was a ferocious, fearsome demon, with trident in hand. The giant *asura* was known as Vritra. Then ensued a battle between the gods and the demons. Vritra was attacked by gods with many kinds of weapons, but the demon nullified their assaults. Then Indra and other gods approached Vishnu for help.

Indra: Lord Vishnu! Vritra, a giant *asura*, is giving us a tough fight, and we are on the verge of defeat. We seek your intervention and help.

Vishnu: What is the immediate provocation for this battle?

Indra: Vritra is a terrible demon. He has stolen the water, and appropriated it to himself as also to his army of *asuras*. The earthlings are in great distress owing to the scarcity of water.

Lord Vishnu: Go to sage Dadhichi. Tell him the whole story. Take him into confidence. He will certainly help, especially when you tell him that the demon has stolen the entire water. His body is strong and hard owing to many years of *tapasya*. Ask him for his body. He will not refuse. He is charitable by nature; always ready to make sacrifices for the well-being of others. You can make a weapon, called *vajra*, from Dadhichi's bones. You will kill demon Vritra with this *vajra*.

Indra: Rishi Dadhichi! We have been sent by Lord Vishnu. Presently a battle is going on between the *asuras* and the *devas*. *Asura* Vritra has stolen water, leaving all the creatures of the earth thirsty and hungry. The giant demon is so powerful that the demigods are likely to be defeated by him. Lord Vishnu has told us that a *vajra* made out of your bones, will kill Vritra.

Dadhichi: Since you have been sent by Lord Vishnu, I will not refuse to grant you your wish. For the mere physical body is nothing. It is the *atma* (soul) inside the body that is everything. Moreover, the cause is noble, which is the freeing of the water. I am willing to sacrifice my life for this noble cause.

Gunadhya: Sage Dadhichi used his yogic powers; his soul left his body, leaving him dead. The gods requested Vishvakarma, the architect of the *devas*, to fashion a *vajra* out of the bones of sage Dadhichi. With *vajra* Indra attacked Vritra and his army of *asuras*. The demons were routed; they took to their heels.

Vritra: (*Addressing the demons deserting the battle field and fleeing*) Cowards! You are demons; brave and strong. Why are you running away? Everyone who is born is destined to die. It is better to die a glorious death in the battle field than die as a coward. Stop fleeing, return!

Gunadhya: But the *asura*-soldiers did not listen. They ran away. However, Vritra continued to fight alone.

Vritra: Indra! I will kill you with my trident, and avenge Vishvarupa's death. But since you have been blessed by Lord Vishnu, you will in all probability kill me with your *vajra*.

Gunadhya: The demon hurled the trident at Indra. But Indra cut it with his *vajra*. And eventually killed Vritra. The demigods were mighty pleased. The credit for the victory of the demigods, went to *Rishi* Dadhichi, who donated his bones to defeat the evil. Dadhichi sacrificed his life, so that gods might live in peace.

# EPILOGUE

The *Vedic* and the post-*vedic* era were an age of seers and saints, who did *tapasya* on the mountains, in the forests, for years and years. It was an age of *ashrams* where was imparted both temporal and spiritual education. It was an age of piety, of religion, of simplicity. The *ashrams* were interspersed in the entire length and breadth of the country. The basic needs of the common populace were not many. They were largely confined to food, shelter and clothing. By and large, people were forest dwellers; they lived in the lap of the nature, in the pollution-free environment, drinking clean water, breathing fresh air. It was an age of serenity, of tranquility, of ease, and not of opulence. The yardstick to measure the richness of a person was the number of cows, and or horses, he had. Hence the prefixes "goswami,"and "Ashwapati," with the names of persons.

*Rishis* did *tapasya* not for self-gain, but for the yeoman's service. The relations between the saints and the people were homely, of mutual understanding, of mutual comforts. But there was one person who was generally uncomfortable. He was Lord Indra. Whenever he found a sage engrossed in severe penance for years and years, he felt cramps of discomfiture. He used all tricks and stratagems to break his *tapasya*. The one bold example is that of *Rishi* Vishwamitra. He sent *apsara* Menaka to obstruct and impede the *tapasya* of the sage.

Yet another example is sage Dadhichi. Dadhichi is said to have been a master of a *Vedic* art known as *Brahamvidya*. This ancient *Vedic* spiritual art enabled a man to attain immortality. Indra, the king of demigods, felt that his position was insecure with such power in the hands of a mortal man, especially Dadhichi who possessed great power by virtue of his penance. So, Indra disliked Dadhichi, and wanted to destroy him and his art. He announced that if Dadhichi taught this art to anyone, he would kill the sage. Aswin twins wanted to learn this art. So, they devised a plan to protect the sage from Indra's power. They learned the art of *Brahamvidya* from Dadhichi, and thereafter cut off his head, preserved it, and replaced the original head with the head of a horse. Indra, blinded by wrath, beheaded the horse-headed sage and left. The Ashwin twins then replaced Dadhichi's original head to the beheaded body and revived the sage with the help of the *Brahamvidya*, which he had taught them. Because of this happening, the sage came to be called Ashvashira, that is the one with the head of a horse.

Indra was driven out of *Devloka* by an *asura*, named Vritra. The demon was the personification of drought. He had stolen the water thereby leaving all the creatures of earth in great anguish and despair. He would not release water to the earthlings. When Indra told Dadhichi about Vritra's savage and monstrous act, he readily agreed to help the demigods to kill the demon. For this he offered his bones. He did this act of bountiful magnanimity for freeing the water for all that exists on the earth: man, birds, beast, and nature. There is no gainsaying the fact that sacrificing life for freeing the waters for mankind, is a great act of munificence, of philanthropy, which made Dadhichi as one of the most revered saints of India.

*****

# 10. RISHI BHARADWAJA: AN INTELLECTUAL GIANT

## DRAMATIS PERSONAE

GUNADHYA: The Narrator

RISHI BHARADWAJA: A renowned seer

INDRA: Chief of demigods

A DEMON: Vaarasikha

DIVODASA: A king in ancient India

PUPIL: One

PUPIL: Two

# RISHI BHARADWAJA: AN INTELLECTUAL GIANT

## PROLOGUE

The *Vedic* and post-*Vedic* scriptures as well as the classical literature are replete with sages who were the personifications of phenomenal wisdom. In fact, they were spiritual wizards, who could create miracles with the help of supernatural powers. One such sage was *Rishi* Bharadwaja. He was a seer with poly-dimensional intellect. He contributed many hymns in the *Rig Veda*, especially in the sixth *Mandala*. In addition to that he made immense contribution to science, engineering, economics and literature. He was also a well-known physician who finds a mention in the *Charak Samhita* (a treatise on medicines). The great Kautilya (Chanakya) mentions sage Bharadwaja seven times in his famous book, *Arthshastra*. Obviously, Chanakya had great respect for the economic-tenets of Bharadwaja. There are several texts, treatises and compositions which are attributed to this sage. The chapter on *dhanurvidya* in the *Mahabharata* is believed to have been written by Bharadwaja, and is deemed to be an *upveda* on archery. He is also renowned to have written such texts as *Bharadwaja Samhita, Bharadwaja Straut-sutra and Grihyasutra. Bharadwaja Shiksha* is an ancient Sanskrit treatise on *phonetics and niti-shastra;* it is a treatise on ethics and practical conduct. He is also stated to have written *Pushan Samhita,* which deals with Pushan cult. Pushan was a *Vedic* deity who was revered by shepherds and cowherds. Bharadwaja propounded that Pushan protected and proliferated milch-cattle, especially the cows, and saved them from being stolen by the thieves. And the most significant contribution of sage Bharadwaja is *Vimana Shastra*, a treatise on the science of aviation. It is an ancient Sanskrit text on aerospace technology. This treatise confirms the existence of aircrafts in India centuries ago. *Rishi* Bharadwaja was as prolific an author as *Rishi* Ved Vyasa. There is no gainsaying the fact that sage Bharadwaja was a multi-faceted intellect whose contribution to the fields of science, engineering, art, medicines, etc., was manifold.

## CURTAIN RAISER

My name is Gunadhya. I am a celestial being. I came to the earth in the world of mortals as a story-teller. I was the narrator of tales in Somdeva's *Kathasaritasagara (KATHA-SARITA-SAGARA),* that is the Ocean of Stories. And I am going to perform the same role of a narrator in telling the story of Rishi Bharadwaja, a saint of sublime intellect and scholarship, whose contribution to the holy scriptures, and the public-oriented treatises, is immense. The classical literature described him as the greatest and the most learned among ascetics endowed with long life.

There is an interesting legend about his birth. The sage Ucathya had, from his wife, Mamata, a son who was called Dirgha-tamas. This Dirgha-tamas was born blind. Brihaspati, Ucathya's younger brother, is said to have consorted with Mamata. Out of this union was born Bharadwaja, later on known as son of Brihaspati and Mamata. That there was a Rishi called *Drightamas Aucathya Mamateya,* who was blind, is confirmed by the *Rig Veda*. In the

*Mahabharata*, there appears an interesting legend. When Bharadwaja was born to Mamata from Brihaspati, the parents (that is Mamata and Brihaspati) pressed each other to protect the child with the words "*bharad vajam imam.*" Hence the name Bharadwaja is composed of two Sanskrit words: "bhara (d)" and "vaja (m)" which together mean "one who brings nourishment," or "one who protects all."

In the *Mahabharata*, there is yet another legend about *Rishi* Bharadwaja. He was living on the banks of river Ganga. Once an *apsara* (celestial nymph), named Ghritachi, appeared there. At the sight of the *apsara*, the semen of sage Bharadwaja dropped down, which was collected in a cup of leaves (*dona, or drona* in Sanskrit). From this seed was born a son who was named Drona. Later on, this same Drona became the famous Dronacharya, a preceptor of the Pandava and the Kaurava brothers, in the *Mahabharata*. Therefore, Bharadwaja was the father of Dronacharya, and grandfather of Ashwathama. In the *Mahabharata*, Dronacharya is repeatedly referred as Bharadwaja- *putra*, that is son of Bharadwaja.

## ACT: ONE

## SCENE: 1

Gunadhya: Sage Bharadwaja had an insatiable desire to learn. He spent all his time to understand the Vedas. There appears an interesting story in the *Taittirya Brahamana*: "The sage Bharadwaja had tried hard to master all the *Vedas* during the three life-time of hundred years each, which he had secured through the grace of Indra. (*Three life-time simply means a long life*). But all that he could learn during that life-period was, as demonstrated by

Indra, just an atom of a handful taken from the three mountains, which were really the *Vedas*."

Sage Bharadwaja observed rigorous austerities for years, which resulted in the weakening of his body. Eventually, he became so weak that he could hardly sit. Finally, Bharadwaja fell down while meditating. But Indra manifested himself, and saved him.

Indra: What would you do if I grant you another life?

Bharadwaja: I would again perform *tapasya* (penance), this time harder *tapasya,* till I learn more about the *Vedas*.

Indra: *Rishi* Bharadwaja! This is your third life. You spent the last two lives in understanding the *Vedas*. But all that you could learn during that life-time was just a handful taken from the three mountains. The *Vedas* are like the three mountains – vast and deep – but what you have learnt is equal to three handfuls. Nevertheless, I do not discount your sincere efforts. Of course, you have gained more knowledge than the demigods. This is no mean achievement. *Vedic* knowledge is endless. However, gaining the knowledge is quite important, but spreading this knowledge is of greater importance.

Bharadwaja: (*Undaunted by his failure, the intrepid sage said*): I know my limitations. But I would continue to study and master the *Vedas*.

Indra: I am greatly pleased with your devotion. But at the same time, I must tell you that it is well-nigh impossible to master the *Vedas* in the normal way, for the *Vedas* are infinite.

Bharadwaja: Lord Indra! Show me the way I should go about to achieve this aim of my life.

Indra: I advise you to propitiate Lord Shiva. With His blessings, you would be able to master the *Vedas*.

Gunadhya: The *Taittirya Brahamana* dilates on a story as to how the divinities imparted to king Janaka the secret of *Savitra-vidya*, which is said to have the efficacy of removing all sins and hurdles in giving long life, and with the help of this *vidya*, a person secures a place in the heaven. Acting on the advice of Indra, and blessed by Lord Shiva, sage Bharadwaja, hence onwards, decided to spread the *Vedic* knowledge among all the people. He made all out efforts to free the society from poverty, disease and war. For this purpose, as also for spreading the *Vedic* knowledge, he travelled far and wide. Many people, including kings, became his disciples. King Divodasa, who is repeatedly mentioned in the *Vedas*, was one of them.

## SCENE: 2

Gunadhya: Sage Bharadwaja had a halo of divinity. He was one of those *Rishis* who were able to communicate with the deities. Once it so happened that sage Bharadwaja had invited Lord Indra, Lord Agni (god of fire), and Soma (the moon god) for a *yajna*. The sage's wife had put milk and rice on fire for *kheer* to be served to gods and other guests after the *yajna*. When the steam started coming out of the pot, suddenly there emerged out of the pot a human-like creature. Sage Bharadwaja was informed of the strange happening. He came running to the spot. But before he could reach the pot, the mysterious figure, that had emerged out of the steam, to everybody's surprise, had eaten the whole of the *kheer*.

Bharadwaja: Who are you? And how and why have you come here?

Demon: I am a demon. My name is Vaarasikha. I have the permission from Lord Brahma to destroy every *yajna* being organized anywhere on the earth.

Bharadwaja: I request you to bless the *yajna*, rather than destroy it.

Demon: Sage! I respect and regard you. Instead of getting annoyed at my conduct, you are pliant and deferential. I must tell you my story. I was wicked and avaricious, and constantly harassed people with my sons and a large army. We had learnt an excellent art of preventing ourselves with an invisible protective armor. Lord Brahma was annoyed with our wickedness. He cursed me. And I became what I am today. Reverend sage! If you sprinkle a few drops of *amrit* (nectar) on me, I will be liberated from this curse.

Bharadwaja: I cannot do that. *Amrit* is the property of the gods. They had worked hard to churn the ocean to obtain the nectar. Therefore, I cannot get *amrit* from the demigods for the sake of freeing a demon from the curse. Ask for something else which is in my power to grant.

Demon: In the alternative, I beseech you to sprinkle the holy water of the Ganga. The water of the Ganga is equal to the nectar, and so also gold and ghee extracted from the milk of cows. If these things are sprinkled on me, then I will be relieved of the curse. And in that eventuality, I will bless the *yajna*.

Gunadhya: The kind-hearted sage performed the *abhishekam* (offered the three things) with all the three, Gangajal, gold and ghee from the cows' milk. This helped the demon. He got liberated from the curse. Then he blessed the *yajna,* which was completed without any hassle.

## SCENE: 3

Gunadhya: There was a king named Divodasa. He is mentioned in the *Rig Veda* as a pious, liberal king. According to the scriptures, "he was a very liberal sacrificer." He was also called *Atithi-gwa – i.e., he to whom guests should go.* Sage Bharadwaja was the priest of Divodasa. This hypothesis is supported by the *Mahabharata,* where it is mentioned: "Bharadwaja went from Vaishali to Kashi, and became the priest of Divodasa." It is also believed that the sage had performed a *yajna*, and as a result of that sacrifice, king Divodasa was blessed with a son, named Pratardana. A legend has it that once Divodasa was attacked by *asuras* (demons). It was a fierce battle between the demons and the forces of the king. The demons destroyed dwellings, plundered the properties, and cut the heads of men, women and children. Divodasa's army was routed. He came running to Bharadwaja.

Divodasa: Rishi! In the battle with the demons, my army has got a serious drubbing. Whatever little remains of my forces, we want to seek shelter in your hermitage to escape total massacre.

Bharadwaja: King! You are a coward. There is no place for cowards in my *ashram.* Go and fight against the *asuras* with your depleted army. A king should be brave enough to fight against all odds and win the bout. King! it is your bounden duty to save your countrymen. Even if you sacrifice your life in the fight, it is worthwhile and justifiable.

Divodasa: Sire! I am not a coward. I have come to request you to perform a *yajna* to propitiate gods to help me win the war. There is a great power in Mantras. Recitation of Mantras in the *yajna* will certainly contribute to my victory.

Gunadhya: Sage Bharadwaja performed the victory *yajna*. Divodasa eventually defeated the *asura* army and won the battle.

## SCENE: 4

Gunadhya: According to several references scattered in the *Vedas*, it appears that the clan of Rishi Bharadwaja was most devoted to the *Pushan* cult. Pushan is a deity frequently mentioned in the *Vedas*. Many hymns are addressed to him. The word Pushan comes from the root "push," which primarily means "nourisher." According to the *Taittiriya Brahmana*: "When Prajapati formed living creatures, Pushan nourished them." Rishi Bharadwaja was so much influenced by the Pushan cult that he wrote *Pushan Samhita*, a treatise on the subject. His pupils in his hermitage were inquisitive about Pushan cult, and wanted to know and understand as to what it is all about!

Pupil One: Guruji! You have written *Pushan Samhita*, a treatise on the Pushan cult. What is this cult? We want to know about it. Please explain it to us.

Bharadwaja: My clan has been closely associated with the ancient *Vedic* tribes. Their main occupation has been cattle breeding. Pushan was the patron god of these nomadic cowherd and shepherds. The living Pushan cult can very well be realized from the *Pushan Samhita.*

Pupil Two: We have a large number of milch cows in our *ashram.* Please explain this cult with reference to the cows.

Bharadwaja: The *Rig Veda* propounds, and I also believe, that cows with calves should ever be in the house. Then there is an advice that the cows may never be lost, or injured, or stolen by robbers. The cows are essential for our lives. Their milk strengthens a weakling, and also endows an ugly man with beauty. A feeling of disgust towards the slaughter of cows has been suggested in the *Rig Veda.*

Pupil One: And what role does Pushan play?

Bharadwaja: Pushan is a protector, a multiplier of cattle, and of human possession in general. As cowherd he gives an ox-goad (goad is a pointed stick for driving oxen, *ankush*), and he is drawn by goats instead of horses.

Gunadhya: Pushan is a god belonging to a world more or less different from that of many Vedic gods. Pushan played a prominent role in the pastoral life of the people. He increases the cattle, and brings back the beasts which have strayed. He bears the goad which is typical of a shepherd, or a cowherd. He is the Lord of paths and helps nomadic tribes in their ways. He bestows great bounty on his followers, particularly in the form of increase in cattle.

## EPILOGUE

The sages of ancient India were highly learned persons. But *Rishi* Bharadwaja stands tall amongst all of them. He was a sharp intellect personified, a saint of great scholarship. He was the knower of the *Vedas*. Verily, there were times in ancient times when knowledge was not what appeared to the senses, but what was revealed in the mystic moments when the Self found itself one with Supreme. And thus, begot an experiential process called "vedi," that is to know. The word Veda is derived from the root "vedi," which means divine knowledge, an illimitable store-house of all education, an inexhaustible mine of the profoundest wisdom - spiritual, secular and temporal -needed by mankind. Sage Bharadwaja tried to master this knowledge embedded in the *Vedas*.

He is believed to have lived a very long life. Though he belongs to the *Vedic* era, he was still there when Lord Rama visited his ashram. In the *Ramayana*, Rama, Sita and Lakshmana, meet sage Bharadwaja in his hermitage at the start of their fourteen-year exile. The seer requests them to stay at his *ashram* and spend the exile-duration there. But Rama reverentially declines the suggestion, and expresses a desire to go deeper in the forest. It was here that sage Bharadwaja tells Rama the way to Chitrakuta. Again, it was at Bahardwaja's hermitage that Bharat and Sumanth reach in search of Rama to bring him back to Ayodhya. Rishi Bharadwaja is said to have blessed Rama while he was returning from Lanka.

The legend mentioned in the *Ramayana* states that Bharadwaja was a disciple of Valmiki, and was a witness to Valmiki's spontaneous utterance of a stanza *"ma nishad,"* etc. The *Yogavasishta* tells us that Valmiki narrated the legend in the first part of the *Ramayana* first to Bharadwaja.

****

# 11.RISHI KASHYAPA: A PROGENITOR OF DEVAS AND ASURAS

## DRAMATIS PERSONAE

GUNADHYA: The Narrator

RISHI KASHYAPA: A renowned seer

ADITI: Wife of Kashyapa: *Devmata* (Mother of demigods)

DITI: Sage Kasyapa's wife: mother of *asura*s

KARDU: Wife of Sage Kashyapa

VINATA: Wife of *Rishi* Kashyapa

VISHNU: Lord God, the Preserver

BRAHMA: GOD OF CREATION

VALI: A demon king, and the grand-father of Prahlad

SHUKRACHARYA: The preceptor pf demons

INDRA: Chief of demigods

NAGAS: Serpents

GARUDA: A mythical bird

# *RISHI* KASHYAPA: A PROGENITOR OF *DEVAS* AND *ASURAS*

## PROLOGUE

Who is a *Rishi*? A Rishi is a person who has *drishti*, who has the spiritual vision to see time past, time present and time future. He is the one who is endowed with a prophetic knowledge. And what he sees through his intuitive knowledge is the *Veda*. Interestingly, the word Veda is linguistically connected with the Latin "video," that is to see. The sages who 'see' the religio-spiritual knowledge, embedded in the holy scriptures, are seers, that is *rishis*.

Sage Kashyapa is one such *Rishi*, a seer most distinguished and most celebrated. He is a highly revered sage. The socio-historical importance of this *Vedic* Rishi is hugely significant, for he is the progenitor of both the *devas* (demigods) and the *asuras* (demons).

Every sage in the Hindu mythology is a highly learned person. And sage Kashyapa is no exception. He is the author of a notable treatise, *Kashyap Samhita, or Braddha Jivakiya Tantra*, which is considered to be a classical reference book on *Ayurveda*, especially in the fields of *Ayurvedic* Pediatrics, Gynecology, and Obstetrics.

He happens to belong to an illustrious family. He is a descendent of Lord Brahma. His father, sage Marichi, was a *manas-putra* (mind-born son) of Brahma. He had married thirteen daughters of

Daksha Prajapati. So, his wives Aditi, Diti and Vinata, among others, were the sisters of Sati, the consort of Lord Shiva. Aditi was the *Devmata* (mother of demigods). Lord Indra was her son. And most importantly, Lord Vishnu in His fifth avatar as Vamana, was also her son. And from Diti were born *asuras* (demons) Hiranyakashipu, and Hiranyaksh. Sage Kashyapa was the grand-father of Prahlad, the staunch devotee of Lord Vishnu.

## CURTAIN RAISER

My name is Gunadhya. I am a celestial being. I came to the earth in the world of mortals as a story-teller. I was the narrator of tales in Somdeva's *Kathasaritasagara (KATHA-SARITA-SAGARA)* That is the Ocean of Stories. And I am going to perform the same role of a narrator in telling the story of *Rishi* Kashyapa, a great seer of the *Vedic* and the post-*Vedic* era.

Kashyapa, alternatively *Kachhapa*, means tortoise in Sanskrit. Perhaps, it has some connection with the *Kurma* avatar of Lord Vishnu. He is one of the *saptarshi* (seven *Rishis*). He is considered to be the author of several hymns in the *Rig Veda*. He is also mentioned as the earliest *Rishi* in the colophon verse of the *Brihadaranyka Upanishad,* one of the oldest *upanishadic* scriptures. Several legends propound that Kashmir got its name from sage Kashyapa. The name Kashmir is a shortened form of "Kashyapa Mir," or the lake of sage Kashyapa. Alternatively, historians believe that Kashmir derives its name from "Kashyapa Meru," that is the sacred mountains of Kashyapa.

Kashyapa is repeatedly mentioned in the *Puranas*, as also in the later classical literature, the *Ramayana* and the *Mahabharata*. For example, in the *Mahabharata*, and in the *Vishnu Purana*, he is described to have married thirteen daughters of Daksha Prajapati. Daksha (literally means "able, competent, intelligent") was the mind-born son (*manas putra*) of Lord Brahma. The names of the thirteen wives of sage Kashyapa, were Aditi, Diti, Kadru, Danu, Arishta, Surasa, Vinata, Tamra, Krodhavasa, Ida, Khasa, Yamini and Muni. Three of his wives – Aditi, Diti and Vinata -- played a significant role in molding the socio-historical and religio-spiritual history of ancient India. Aditi was *Devmata*, mother of all gods, including Indra, while Diti gave birth to demons like Hiranyakashipu and Hiranyaksh. Aditi was also the mother of Lord Vishnu in his dwarf incarnation (Vaman Avatar). And Vinata was the mother of Garuda (a mythical bird), and the vehicle of Lord Vishnu. That is why Garuda is generally referred to as Vinata.

## ACT: ONE

## SCENE: 1

Gunadhya: One evening *Rishi* Kashyapa had almost finished his day's worship and meditation, and was adding the last offering to the sacrificial fire. The sun had almost set. It was twilight. The dusk was approaching fast. At that time, his wife, Diti, approached him.

Diti: Swami! I have an ardent desire to have children. I want you to fulfill my desire.

Kashyapa: Diti! The evening is not an auspicious time for cohabitation to implant the seed for children. I must tell you that as soon as the dusk falls, goblins and demons come out of their hiding and wander around on the earth. To think of making any endeavor to have a child at this time, will be in conflict with, and in defiance of the socio-religious norms and practices.

Diti: What is right or wrong, I don't care! Willy-nilly, I want a son.

Kashyapa: Diti! You have disturbed me in my prayers. I am already late in making the last offering to the sacrificial fire. I have to finish my evening worship and prayer soon enough. I know you are desirous of having a son. Please wait for another hour. Presently, it is time for Rudra to be accompanied by *pisachas* (goblins). Please keep your mind away, for some time, from the worldly pleasures. And let me worship the Lord with pure mind.

Gunadhya: But Diti would not listen to her sage-husband. She insisted on her desire.

Kashyapa: Diti! You are compelling me to commit an act of dereliction. Since I am morally bound to you, I have no alternative except to pave the way for your wish.

Gunadhya: After the act, sage Kashyapa bathed in the cool water, and sat again for the prayer and the meditation.

## SCENE: 2

Diti: Swami! I am ashamed of my conduct to force

you to fulfill my desire. I beg your pardon. I supplicate to Rudra (Lord Shiva) to forgive me and save and protect the seed the sage has planted in my womb. I also beseech Lord Shiva to listen to my solicitation and protect me and my coming generation.

Kashyapa: Diti! Your remorse is misplaced. It was actually so ordained. Your wrong has been two-fold. First, you have been a victim of your own desire. And second, you disobeyed your husband's advice, and refused to pay heed to his words. So, you will be giving birth to two sons (twins) of extremely bad nature and wicked character. They will murder the innocent people, violate the chastity of women, humiliate saints and ascetics, and even challenge Lord Vishnu. However, when their wicked deeds proliferate beyond tolerance, Lord Vishnu will himself be incarnated to kill them.

Diti: I regret my mistake. Please take pity on me, and annul what is ordained for the still-to-be born sons.

Gunadhya: Eventually were born two sons in Kashyapa's *ashram*. They were twins, named Hiranyakashipu and Hiranyaksh. The legend of these two brothers goes back to the heaven. One day four Sanatkumaras (sages), Lord Brahma's mind-born sons, visited Lord Vishnu in *Vaikuntha*. But they were stopped at the gate by two gatekeepers, Jaya and Vijaya. Angered by their audacity, the sages cursed them to be born on the earth into the world of lust, anger and greed. Thus, Hiranyakashipu and Hiranyaksh were, in fact, Jaya and Vijaya, who were ousted from the heaven, and thrown on the earth to be born as demons. Both the demons were highly wicked who perpetrated atrocities on the denizens of the earth.

Kashyapa: Diti! Your remorse has engendered pity in me. In our family will be born a grandson who will be a staunch devotee of Lord Vishnu. This will compensate you for your woes.

Gunadhya: Both Hiranyakahipu and Hiranyaksh were eventually killed by Lord Vishnu; Hiranyakashipu by His Narsimha avatar, and Hiranyaksh by His Boar incarnation. Prahlad was the son of Hiranyakashipu. He was a devotee of Lord Vishnu. After the death of his father, he ascended to the throne. After him, his son, Virochana became the king. He was a kind-hearted and righteous ruler. When sage Sanatkumara taught him about the truth of this world, he abdicated his throne, and made his son, Vali, a king of the demons in his place.

## SCENE: 3

Gunadhya: There was a sage named Sanatakumara (a mind-born son of Brahma). Once he visited king Virochana, son of Prahlada. Virochana was pleased to meet the sage. The sage instructed the king about the true nature of the universe. The discourse and teachings of the sage so impressed king Virochana, that he abdicated his throne, went off to the forest for meditation and *tapasya*, after having crowned his son, Vali, as the king of the demons. Vali was a good and righteous king, devoted to the well- being of his subjects.

Eventually, it so happened that king Vali defeated Indra and other gods in a fierce battle, and won over heaven from them. The demigods were thrown out of their heavenly kingdom. Aditi, the mother of all gods

(*Devmata)* became despondent seeing her children lose their kingdom, and suffering at the hands of the demons. She prayed to Lord Vishnu for help.

Vishnu: *Devmata!* You have propitiated me. Please ask for the boon.

Aditi: There is a demon, named Vali, who is the descendant of Hiranyakashipu, father of Prahlada. He has defeated demigods, my sons, and has driven them out of heaven. The demons are oppressing my children. Please grant me a son who will defeat the demons and restore the heaven to my sons.

Vishnu: *Devmata!* Do not despair. I myself will be born as your son. I will deal with the demons in the manner and to the extent appropriate and to your satisfaction.

Gunadhya: Lord Vishnu was born as Aditi's son. He was born as a dwarf. This was Lord Vishnu's Vamana avatar (incarnation). He studied Vedas under the sage Bharadwaja.

Meanwhile Vali, the demon king, had organized a *yajna.* Lord Vishnu, in the guise of a dwarf, came to participate in the ceremony.

Vali: Soldiers! Please make announcement all over the kingdom that I will not refuse anything anybody asks. Shukracharya! You are my preceptor, my guru, please bless me and my *yajna.*

Gunadhya: As soon as king Vali saw the dwarf, he welcomed him to his *yajna,* and paid him obeisance.

Shukracharya: Vali! I visualize that this dwarf will hoodwink you, because in the form of a dwarf, he is none other than Vishnu himself. I, therefore, warn you to be on your guard. Do not grant what he asks for.

Vali: Vishnu is the Lord of everything. I am indeed fortunate if Vishnu has come to grace my ceremony in the guise of a dwarf. How can I refuse what he demands!

Gunadhya: Notwithstanding the warning given by his preceptor, Shukracharya, Vali welcomed the dwarf.

Vali: What is your desire? What do you want? I am duty bound to fulfill your wish.

Vishnu: Rajan! I desire nothing much. I do not want gold or riches, elephants or horses. All that I ask for is as much of land as can be covered by three footsteps of mine.

Vali: This is nothing. Your wish is granted. Measure the land with your three steps; it will be yours.

## SCENE: 4

Gunadhya: As soon as Vali uttered these words, the dwarf assumed a gigantic form. His head rose way up into the sky. With each of his step Vishnu covered the entire *triloki* (all the three worlds). With one step, he covered the entire earth. With the second he covered the entire sky. And with the third and the final step, he covered the entire heaven.

The entire universe is inside an egg *(anda)*, and outside the egg there is water. Vishnu's foot cracked the shell of the egg, and some of the water that was outside, flowed. The water began to gush out through the sky, which became the heavenly Ganga, that is the Milky Way.

Thus, Vali ended up by donating all of the three worlds to Vishnu, and there was nowhere for him to live in.

Vishnu: (*Having traversed all the land that was available, Lord Vishnu assumed His form of a dwarf*). Vali! You have donated all the three worlds to me. Where will you stay now?

Vali: Lord! I seek refuge with you.

Vishnu: Go and live in the underworld. As for the heaven, I restore it to Indra and other gods, and thus fulfill my promise made to *Devmata* Aditi.

Aditi: I bow before you Lord Vishnu! You have relieved me and my children of great distress and despondency. You have taught a mighty lesson to demon Vali for his ill-deeds.

## SCENE: 5

Gunadhya: Among the thirteen daughters of Daksha Prajapati, who were married to sage Kashyapa, besides Aditi and Diti, were Kadru and Vinata. There is an interesting legend appertaining these two women. The story has it that one day sage Kashyapa asked them for a boon.

Kashyapa: Kadru and Vinata! I am pleased with the way you have served me. I want to reward you for your *seva* (service). Please tell me what do you want? I will fulfill your wish.

Kadru: I want a son who is courageous and brave.

Vinata: I want two sons who are potent and commanding.

Kashyapa: *Tathastu*! Be it so. I give both of you two eggs each. Those eggs will engender the progeny you want.

Gunadhya: Out of the eggs of Kadru were born n*agas* (serpents). But Vinata, out of jealousy, broke one egg prematurely. Out of the broken egg emerged an undeveloped child, whose upper part was fully developed, while the lower part remained undeveloped. That child, when born, cursed his mother that she would become a vassal of Kadru. But he added a proviso that if out of the second egg a fully developed child is born, he will free his mother from the curse of slavery. The first child, named Arun, became a charioteer of the sun. And the second child became Garuda, a mythical bird, who flew away into the sky.

## SCENE: 6

Gunadhya: One day Kadru and Vinata went out for a long walk. Both of them saw a horse grazing at a distance. They entered into an argument over the exact colour of the horse.

Vinata: The colour of the horse is white.

Kadru: Yes! the colour of the horse is white, but its tail is black.

Gunadhya: The altercation turned into a verbal duel. Kadru hazarded a bet, that one who loses the wager will serve the other as a slave. Kadru disliked

Vinata. So, she embarked on a strategy to dupe her.

Kadru: My *naga* sons! I entrust to you a simple errand. Go and encircle the tail of yonder horse so that it looks black. I will, thus, win the bet, defeating Vinata.

Gunadhya: The serpents did what their mother asked them to do. Next day when both Kadru and Vinata went to have a look at the horse, they found its tail black. So, Vinata became a vassal of Kadru as per the condition of the bet. Vinata was very angry. She could see through the fraud.

Vinata: Serpent sons of Kadru! You have hoodwinked me. For this serious dereliction I curse you that you will burn alive in the Janamejaya *yajna*.

Gunadhya: Janamejaya was a renowned king who was the son of Parikshit, and the great grand-son of Arjuna. His father, Parikshit, had died of snake bite. Janamejaya had performed a sacrifice of serpents. He is, thus, called a "serpent sacrificer." Lord Brahma approved of the combustion of serpents. He called sage Kashyapa.

Lord Brahma: Kashyapa! I approve of the combustion of serpents. Your wife did the right thing to curse them. The population of serpents, produced by you, has increased manifold. The curse of your wife has resulted in the reduction of the proliferating number of *nagas*. Therefore, do not be angry with Vinata. However, I give you the Mantra to cure the people of the poison of snake bite.

## SCENE: 7

Gunadhya: Garuda was deeply concerned about the

servitude of his mother. Since *nagas* were responsible for her servility, he thought of approaching them to help free her mother from bondage.

Garuda: *Nagas*! Please tell me what should I do to free my mother, Vinata, from the slavery of your mother.

Nagas: Please bring *amrit* (nectar) for us to enable us to defeat death.

Gunadhya: Garuda embarked on the search for *amrit*. He reached heaven. There he found that two serpents were guarding the pot of nectar. Garuda killed them and took the pot of nectar. But he did not drink *amrit* himself.

Vishnu: Garuda! I am pleased with your sense of abnegation. I, therefore, grant you a boon that without drinking *amrit*, you will remain immortal. I also grant your prayer, and make you my vehicle.

Indra: (*On his return journey, Garuda was accosted by Indra)*. Garuda! Please give this *amrit* pot to me. If the serpents drink it, they will become deathless, and will cause serious hurt to the world.

Garuda: Lord Indra! I see convincing reasons in your advice. Therefore, I give this *amrit kalash* to you.

Indra: I grant you the boon that hence onwards serpents will become your food.

Gunadhya: Garuda then came to the *nagas*. He told them that he had brought the nectar pot, and had kept it at the *kusha* grass (a seat made of grass). He then proposed that the *nagas* should free Vinata, his mother, from servility. Which the serpents did. He then told them to go and bathe in the cool water and then drink nectar. *Nagas* ran to a pool to bathe. Garuda freed his mother. When *Nagas* returned, they did not find the nectar pot. They only licked the *kusha* grass, which cut their tongues into two parts. Since then, serpents became forked-tongued.

## EPILOGUE

When we talk of the evolution of the earth, and the genesis of all that exists in the world, then we simply mean human beings, animals, birds, nature, vegetation, etc. *Rishi* Kashyapa married thirteen daughters of Daksha Prajapati to proliferate this world of all existence. Scriptures propound that sage Kashyapa was the father of human beings, demons, animals, birds, and so on. Owing to the thirteen wives of Kashyapa, this world multiplied and expanded. Here is a brief delineation of the lineage of sage Kashyapa, qua the entire world.

From Aditi were born the Adityas (celestial beings, of whom Varuna was the chief), demigods, including Indra, and the Vamana avatar of Lord Vishnu (dwarf incarnation). Diti gave birth to Hiranyakashipu and Hiranyaksh, the two demons, and a daughter, Singhika. From Kadru were born *Nagas* (serpents), and Vinata gave birth to Aruna and Garuda. The *Danvas* (demons) were the sons of Danu, and the *apsaras* (celestial nymphs) were born from Muni. From Kashta were born horses, and other hoofed animals. Arishta gave birth to Gandharvas. From Ira were born trees, bushes, and other vegetation. Tamra gave birth to vultures and other carrion birds, Patangi gave birth to birds, Yamini to insects, and so on.

It is believed that Kashmir may have got its name from Kashyapa *Rishi*. According to a legend the vale of Kashmir was a high-altitude lake which was drained by sage Kashyapa, and out of which the beautiful valley of Kashmir emerged. Hence the name Kashyap-mira, which became overtime Kashmir. Kashmir, according to historians, is a shortened form of Kashyapa Mir, which means "lake of the sage Kashyapa." Kashmir is said to be made up of two Sanskrit words, "ka" and "smira", together they mean "the land from which water was drained by "ka", or "Prajapati" (the Lord). Alternatively, it may have come from a Kasshmiri, or Sanskrit term that means "to dry up water." It could also have been derived from the term "Kashyapa Meru," which means the sacred mountains of Kashyapa.

In the ancient texts of Greece, linked to the expedition of Alexander the Great, this land has been called "Kasperia," possibly a contraction of "Kashyapamira." In some *Puranas*, Kashyapa is said to have drained the Kashmir valley to make it inhabitable. This may be an allegory for teaching ideas and doctrines, removing stagnant waters of ignorance, and extending learning and civilization in the valley. This hypothesis stands substantiated from the fact that sage Kashyapa had set up his school and *ashram* on the land that was reclaimed from the water. And this reclaimed land was named after him.

*****

# 12.BHRIGU: THE SAGE WHOSE ARROGANCE WAS HUMBLED BY VISHNU

## DRAMATIS PERSONAE

GUNADHYA: The narrator

BHRIGU: A renowned sage

KAVYAMATA: Sage Bhrigu's wife

LORD VISHNU: The Preserver of the world

SHIVA: Mahadeva

BRAHMA: The God of creation

SHUKRACHARYA: The Guru of Demons

INDRA: A vedic deity

Demons

Sages

# BHRIGU: THE SAGE WHOSE ARROGANCE WAS HUMBLED BY VISHNU

## PROLOGUE

Bhrigu is one of the seven great sages, *Saptrishis*. He is also one of the *Prajapatis,* created by Lord Brahma for the facilitation and maintenance of the creation. According to the *Manusmriti*, sage Bhrigu was a contemporary of Manu, the Hindu progenitor of humanity. He is believed to have lived during the time of Manu.

There is something unique about this seer. He is the famous author of *Bhrigu Samhita*, which is considered as the astrological (*Jyotish*) classic. In fact, sage Bhrigu is the very first compiler of predictive astrology. He was the *manas-putra* (mind-born son) of Lord Brahama. The name Bhargava is used to refer to the descendants of the clan of Bhrigu. Interestingly, the sage had built his *Ashram* close to the Dhosi Hills (presently situated in Mahindergarh district of Haryana, on the Rajasthan – Haryana border).

It is believed that like Manu, Bhrigu too made great contribution to the *Manusmriti*, which comprised the contents of the sermons delivered to the saints. According to the *Skanda Purana*, Bhrigu migrated to Bhrigu-Kutch, modern Bharauch, on the banks of the river Narmada in Gujarat, leaving his son Chyavana, who gave *Chyavan-prash*, a jam-like Ayurvedic preparation, to the world. *Chyavan-prash* is very popular among house-holders. It is believed to improve general health, vitality and immunity.

## CURTAIN RAISER

My name is Gunadhya. I am a celestial being. I came to the earth in the world of mortals as a story-teller. I was the narrator of tales in Somdeva's *Kathasaritasagara (KATHA -SARITA-SAGARA),* that is the Ocean of Stories. And I am going to perform the same role of a narrator in telling the story of *Rishi* Bhrigu, a great seer who gave to the world the knowledge about predictive astrology.

Bhrigu was a great *Vedic* seer who was the founder of the race of Bhrigus, in which was born sages like Jamadagni and Parshuram. In the *Mahabharata,* there appears an interesting legend, which tells us how Bhrigu rescued sage Agastya from the tyranny of king Nahusha. King Nahusha had obtained superhuman power. Bhrigu crept into Agastya's hair to avoid the potent glance of Nahusha, and when that tyrant bound Agastya to his chariot, and kicked him on the head to move faster, Bhrigu cursed Nahusha, and turned him into a python. Bhrigu on Nahusha's supplication limited the duration of the curse. He was freed from the curse when Yudhishtra answered his questions satisfactorily.

Bhrigu belonged to an illustrious family. His lineage goes back to king Daksha. He was married to Khyati, one of the several daughters of Daksha. He had two sons, named Dhata and Vidhata, and one daughter, Lakshmi, who was married to Lord Vishnu. From Kavyamata, he had another son, named Shukracharya, the great sage and the preceptor of the *Asuras* (demons). He is said to have two more sons, sage Chyavana from Puloma, and a folk-hero, Mrikanda. One of *Rishi* Brighu's descendants was sage Jamadagni, who in turn was the father of Parshuram. Such is the great race of Maharshi Bhrigu.

## ACT: ONE

## SCENE: 1

Gunadhya: Almost every legend in the scriptures of India is replete with one or the other curse. Curses are, of course, scary, and one would prefer to avoid them. Yet there are many curses which have positive outcome, and which have changed the course of history, nay of Hindu culture and civilization. One such important curse appertains sage Bhrigu and Lord Vishnu.

The gods and the demons fought all the time, and the demons were sometimes worsted in these encounters. The *Matsya Purana* describes one such terrible war that broke out between the *Devas* (demigods) and *Asuras* (demons). The demons were routed in the battle. Having been defeated, they decided to approach their Guru, Shukracharya, for assistance. Shukracharya consoled the demons.

Shukracharya: Demons! Do not worry. I will undertake severe *tapasya* (penance) to acquire powers which will make the *Asuras* invincible. I am going off to do *tapasya*. While I am gone, do not fight with the gods. Give up arms and lead the lives of hermits. Wait till my return. In the meantime, go to the *ashram* of my father, *Rishi* Bhrigu, and take refuge there.

Gunadhya: Shukracharya did penance to propitiate Lord Shiva. At long last, Shiva manifested Himself to the preceptor of the demons.

Shiva: Shukracharya! I am pleased with your *tapasya*. Please ask for the boon.

Shukracharya: Lord Shiva! Grant me the knowledge of *Mrit Sanjeevni* mantra to enable me to revive the dead demons to life and make them invincible.

Shiva: *Tathastu*! I fulfill your wish and give the *Mrit Sanjeevni* Mantra to you.

## SCENE: 2

Gunadhya: Meanwhile the gods came to know what Shukracharya was up to. They realized that once Shukracharya returned with the *Mrit Sanjeevni* Mantra, it would be well-nigh impossible to defeat the demons. They confabulated together and decided that presently it was the best time to attack demons immediately, when they have given up arms, and were living as hermits. Thus, they started killing the demons. There was panic among *Asuras*. As the sage was also not present in the hermitage, they ran to Shukracharya's mother, sage Bhrigu's wife, for protection.

Demons: Indra! We are unarmed and living as ascetics. It is unbecoming of you to attack us when we have forsaken arms.

Gunadhya: But Indra and other gods refused to listen to their pleas. They continued to attack them. Eventually, Kavyamata, Bhrigu's wife, had to intervene to check the aggression of the *Devas*.

Kavyamata: *Asuras*! Do not despair. I will protect you. I will use my yogic powers to immobilize Indra.

He will not be able to move at all. He will stand there like a statue.

Gunadhya: This happening unnerved the gods. They began to flee. Alarmed thus, they rushed poste-haste to Lord Vishnu to seek his help.

Indra: I have been immobilized by Kavyamata, sage Bhrigu's wife. This she has done to save demons who were on the verge of being annihilated by demigods. We, therefore, supplicate to you to help us tide over the crisis.

Vishnu: Indra! Do not worry. I direct you to enter my body, so that I might be able to save you and other gods.

Kavyamata: I am annoyed with you Indra. So also, with Vishnu. I will burn both of you to ashes if you escalated the battle. Better, retreat immediately.

Indra: Lord Vishnu! What are you waiting for? Can't you see that this woman will destroy both of us. Kill her at once!

Gunadhya: Vishnu summoned up his *Sudarshan Chakra*, and severed Kavyamata's head. The sage Bhrigu was not present at that time. When he returned and found out what had happened, he became furious.

Bhrigu: Lord Vishnu! You have committed the crime of killing a woman. Thus, you have violated the tenets of Dharma. I, therefore, curse you that you would be born several times on the earth, and suffer the pain of birth and death. As regards my wife, I will resurrect her through my spiritual powers.

Gunadhya: Owing to this legendary curse, Vishnu had to take a number of avatars on the earth to endure the worldly pain, and pay the price for killing sage Bhrigu's wife. The curse of Bhrigu, which Vishnu endured, has a huge socio-religious and spiritual significance. Lord Vishnu took several avatars (incarnations), including Rama, Krishna, Parshurama, etc. There is no gainsaying the fact that these incarnations made significant contribution to shape the entire history of our civilization, culture and scriptures. The curse also made Vishnu experience emotions such as love, hatred, and pain of separation.

## SCENE: 3

Gunadhya: There appears a legend in the *Padma Purana* that long ago sages and saints gathered to perform a *yagna* on the bank of river Saraswati. A dispute arose among them as to who was the most superior God from amongst the Trinity (Brahma, Vishnu, Mahesh) best entitled to the homage of the Brahmans. Some voted for Vishnu, while others supported Shiva or Brahma. The arguments intensified. But they could not agree to resolve the discord. Ultimately, they decided unanimously to find out the truth. For this they chose sage Bhrigu. He was asked to test the credentials and the characteristic traits of the *Trimurti*.

Bhrigu: Sages! You have entrusted an exacting task to me to test and pick up a deity who is acceptable to all of us for the offer of the homage. I assure you that I will do your bidding to your satisfaction.

Gunadhya: In order to accomplish the task, Bhrigu decided to test each of the Trinity, one by one. He first called on Lord Shiva. When he reached there, he found Shiva engaged with Parvati, his consort. So, Shiva ignored Bhrigu, and even did not notice his presence. This hurt *Rishi* Bhrigu's ego.

Bhrigu: (*The sage was furious on the behaviour of Shiva. He lost the cool of his mind, and cursed the deity*) Shiva! How dare you exhibit your audacity to ignore my presence. I must punish you for your dereliction. I, therefore, curse you to take the form of *Linga*. I pronounce that hence onwards you will have no offerings presented to you.

## SCENE: 4

Gunadhya: Having thus cursed Lord Shiva, the next destination of Bhrigu was Lord Brahma. When he reached there, he found Brahma surrounded by sages. He was so much inflated with his own importance as to treat Bhrigu with inattention. And Bhrigu was not the type of saint who would tolerate any disregard meted out to him.

Bhrigu: Sire! You have insulted and humiliated me. I am angry with you, father!

Brahma: Bhrigu! You hope to receive reverence from your own father. You may be a great scholar, but you lack the manners. You must learn to honor and respect your elders.

Bhrigu: By disregarding me you have betrayed your real self of being made up of foulness. I, therefore, pronounce that hence onwards you will be excluded from the worship by the Brahamans.

## SCENE: 5

Gunadhya: Sage Bhrigu then wended his way to Lord Vishnu's abode. To his utter surprise, he found the Lord asleep. This made Bhrigu indignant.

Bhrigu: Look at this God! Instead of looking after the world, his primary obligation, he is sleeping. How can the Preserver of the world be so irresponsible to sleep like this? He has not even noticed my presence. He is sloth and sluggishness personified.

Gunadhya: Bhrigu's arrogance was stung. Out of sheer exasperation and irritation, he kicked Vishnu on the chest to wake him up. Vishnu's slumber was disturbed. He woke up, and saw Bhrigu standing before him.

Vishnu: *Maharishi*! I welcome you to my heavenly abode. Let me massage your foot lest it should have been hurt.

Gunadhya: By being respectful, and looking humble before the sage, Lord Vishnu destroyed the third eye of Bhrigu that he had on his feet, which symbolized his ignorance and ego. As soon as the sage's ego was destroyed, he realized his egotistical outbursts with extreme repentance. His arrogance was humbled.

Vishnu: Sage! I feel honored to touch your feet. My physical contact with your feet has made me happy. Your foot-prints will ever stay on my chest.

Bhrigu: Lord! I seek your forgiveness for my arrogant aggression. I am highly pleased with your humility. I now realize your unforeseen goodness. I proclaim that you, Lord Vishnu, are the only deity to be worshipped both by men and gods.

Gunadhya: After this encounter with Vishnu, Bhrigu returned to the sages who had sent him on the mission to test and pick up a deity worthy of receiving the offerings of homage.

Bhrigu: Saints and sages! I declare that Lord Vishnu is the greatest of the Trimurti. It is he who should be worshipped, as after test I have found him to be the most suitable and acceptable for the sacrificial homage.

Sages: After having heard the full report as presented by *Rishi* Bhrigu, we unanimously concur with him. Lord Vishnu will be the presiding deity at the *yagna*.

## EPILOGUE

After the incident of testing the Trinity, Bhrigu decided to write his famous book of astrology, the *Bhrigu Samhita*. The seer collected birth charts, wrote full life predictions, and compiled them together as *Bhrigu Samhita*. This book of predictive astrology is believed to be the first book of its kind in the field of astrology.

Bhrigu had become famous as a revered priest also. He was appointed as one of the officiating priests at Daksha's *yagna*. This *yagna* is extremely important in the scriptural history, because it was at this *yagna* that Daksha had abused and insulted Lord Shiva, exasperated by her father's abusive behavior, Sati, the consort of Shiva, had immolated herself. The death of Sati enraged Shiva. He produced spirits like Virabhadra and Mahakali who destroyed Daksha's *yagna*. Virbhadra punished Bhrigu, the officiating priest. He was thrown on the ground, kicked and his mustache plucked.

Another important legend connected with Bhrigu is the story of Bhrigu *Tirtha*. Bhrigu once performed penance to propitiate Shiva. Shiva, pleased with his *tapasya* manifested himself, and asked the sage for a boon. Bhrigu prayed that the place where he performed his penance should become a holy spot. From that day onwards that place came to be known as Bhrigu *Tirtha*.

*****

# 13.RISHI JAMADAGNI: A WISE AND TALENTED SEER

## DRAMATIS PERSONAE

GUNADHYA: The narrator

JAMADAGNI: A renowned sage

RENUKA: Wife of Jamadagni

PARASHURAMA: Jamadagni's son

RICHIKA: A sage, and father of Jamadagni

SATYAVATI: Mother of Jamadagni

GADHI: A king, and father of Satyavati

VARUNA: A god

KARTA-VIRYA: King of Haihaya dynasty

Mother of Satyavati

# RISHI JAMADAGNI: A WISE AND TALENTED SEER

## PROLOGUE

A Brahman and a descendant of sage Bhrigu, *Rishi* Jamadagni is one of the seven great sages, *Saptrishis*. He is the renowned father of sage Parashurama, who was obedience personified; who obeyed his father and beheaded his own mother. Despite belonging to the clan of sage Bhrigu, who was irascible, and cursed whosoever confronted and annoyed him, Jamadagni, in contrast, remained cool-headed even when provoked. He was a saint of great *satvik* nature, and never used his *yogic* powers, obtained through *tapasya*, to harm or curse any living entity. He was blessed with wonderful progeny. He had five sons, the youngest being Parashurama, who was the sixth incarnation of Lord Vishnu. Both father-and-son duo possessed great intelligence, which transformed them to be saints of great wisdom.

According to the *Mahabharata*, Jamadagni had studied hard and "obtained entire possession of the *Vedas*." In fact, he was an erudite *Vedic* Scholar. He acquired the science of weapons without any formal instruction. His father, sage Richika, is believed to have guided him.

## CURTAIN RAISER

My name is Gunadhya. I am a celestial being. I came to the earth in the world of mortals as a story - teller. I was the narrator of tales in Somdeva's *Kathasaritasagara (KATHA-SARITA-SAGARA)*, that is the Ocean of Stories. And I am going to perform the same role of a narrator in telling the story of *Rishi* Jamadagni, a great seer, respected and eulogized for his wisdom. He hails from an illustrious family of the clan of sage Bhrigu.

There are many legends connected with sage Jamadagni. According to the *Mahabharata*, Rishi Jamadagni once got annoyed with *Surya*, the sun-god, for torching the world with too much heat. The warrior-sage shot several arrows into the sky to terrify the sun-god. The sun-god then appeared before the sage in the guise of a Brahman, and gave him two inventions, sandals and umbrella, to help mankind alleviate and mitigate the heat to some extent.

## ACT: ONE

## SCENE: 1

Gunadhya: The story of Rishi Jamadagni's parentage and birth appears in the *Mahabharata* as also in the *Vishnu Purana*. It is related that sage Richika was an aged person. He demanded in marriage Satyavati, the daughter of Gadhi, king of Kanya-kubja. Gadhi was not willing to marry his daughter to so old a man. But he could not say no directly to the sage for fear of being cursed. So, he used a ruse to turn down the proposal of Richika.

Richika: Rajan! I have come to you with a proposal. I want to marry your daughter, Satyavati.

Gadhi: Sage! I dare not say no to your proposal. But you will have to fulfill one condition, before I give the hand of my daughter in marriage to you.

Richika: What is that?

Gadhi: I demand one thousand horses in return for my daughter. These horses should be swift of foot, and white in colour with black ears.

Gunadhya: *Rishi* Richika was a self-realized saint. He approached god Varuna.

Richika: Varuna! You are the upholder of heaven and earth; you are the king of the universe; master of gods and men, and possessor of illimitable knowledge. I want a favour from you.

Varuna: What is that?

Richika: I want one thousand horses. They should be swift of foot, white in colour with black ears.

Varuna: Your wish is granted.

Gunadhya: Sage Richika presented the horses to king Gadhi. The king was now left with no alternative except to marry his daughter to the aged *Rishi*.

## SCENE: 2

Gunadhya: Satyavati wanted a son. So, she approached her husband, and requested him to perform a *yagna* so that she is blessed with a son. Sage Richika acceded to her desire. After the *Putreshti Yagna* (*Yagna* for a son), he gave *charu* (mess, rice pudding) to Satyavati.

Richika: Here is *charu* for you. This will help you give birth to a son.

Satyavati: Swami! I wish that my mother should also have a son. Please prepare a second bowl of rice pudding for her.

Richika: Here are two bowls of mess. "This is for you, and this is for your mother."

Gunadhya: After having given two bowls of mess (rice pudding), saint Richika went off to the forest for meditation. But Satyavati's mother had different notions. She thought that the mess *(charu)* given to her daughter might have better ingredients.

Mother: Satyavati! Generally, everybody wants a good son for himself. None is keen for obtaining a good brother-in-law. I suspect that your rice pudding is better than that of mine. I am a queen, and I am a *kshatriya*. Therefore, I want a son who should rule the world. He has to be strong and brave. Your son will be a Brahman. He does not have to be that powerful. So, let us exchange our bowls.

Gunadhya: They exchanged the bowls of rice pudding. When sage Richika returned, he heard the whole story about what had happened. He got angry with his wife for messing up the mess.

Richika: Satyavati! Into your bowl I had put the ingredients for a son who would be peaceful and non-violent. We are Brahmans. We want a son who will display the traits of a Brahman. And into your mother's bowl, I had put contents for a son who would be brave and violent as *Kshatriya*. Your father is a *Kshatriya,* and as such your mother should have a son who will behave like a *Kshatriya*. But you have turned everything topsy turvy.

Satyavati: I am sorry. I beg your pardon. What I have done cannot be undone now. But I beseech you, Swami, to bless me with a grandson who should be brave and violent.

Gunadhya: Sage Richika granted his wife's desire. Satyavati gave birth to Jamadagni, and her mother to Vishwamitra, who displayed *Kshatriya* traits. It was Jamadagni's son, Parashurama, who exhibited all the *Kshatriya*-like characteristics. Vishwamitra was Gadhi's son; he was born a *Kshatriya*. But subsequently, he turned out to be Brahman-like, because of his austerities.

## SCENE: 3

Gunadhya: *Rishi* Jamadagni was known to be an authority on the *Vedas;* he always engaged himself in gathering knowledge. He was a great *yogi* who performed severe penance. He approached king Prasena-jit with a proposal to marry his daughter, Renuka. Prasena-jit was a descendant of Raghu dynasty, and an ancestor of Lord Rama. The king being aware of the greatness of sage Jamadagni, he gladly married his daughter to him. Even though Renuka was a princess, she turned out to be an ideal and devoted wife. She gave birth to five sons, the youngest being Parashurama. Renuka's single-minded devotion to her husband was so great that she used to carry an unbaked earthen pot every day to fetch water from the nearby river; and it never broke. One day something strange happened which changed the course of her life.

Jamadagni: Renuka! Go to the river, and bring fresh water for the *Yagna* ritual. But be quick, and come back soon.

Gunadhya: Renuka reached the river. She filled the unbaked earthen pitcher with water as usual, when haply she espied a handsome Gandharva dallying with an *apsara* (celestial nymph) in the river waters. For just a fleeting moment, she was smitten with desire for this handsome youth. The unbaked pot that she was carrying dissolved into the river. She was no longer chaste of mind.

Jamadagni: How is it that Renuka has taken so much time in bringing fresh water from the river for the morning sacrifices. With the help of my yogic powers, I envision as to what had happened, that she is no longer pure of mind. She has lost her chastity.

Gunadhya: In the meantime, Renuka returned without water. Suffering a sense of shame, she looked gloomy and guilt-stricken. Jamadagni was so furious that he asked his eldest son to kill his mother. But he refused. Then he asked the other sons, one by one, in order of their births, to behead their mother, but they too refused to carry out the command of their father.

Jamadagni: You four elder sons! You have the temerity to disobey your sage-father. I, therefore, curse you to turn into stones. Parashurama, my youngest son! I now turn to you. I order you to behead your mother.

Gunadhya: Parashurama was an obedient son, and was also wise by nature. He beheaded his mother with his famous axe.

Parashurama: Father! I have carried out your command. I now bow before you to receive punishment for the sin I have committed by killing my own mother. I am guilty as *matri-ghatak* (mother-killer).

Jamadagni: Parashurama! I am extremely pleased with your *pitri-bhakti* (devotion to your father). Please ask for any boon.

Parashurama: Father! I want two boons.

Jamadagni: Son! tell me, what do you want?

Parashurama: Firstly, forgive my mother for any dereliction, and revive her to life. Secondly, unturn my brothers from stones to life.

Jamadagni: Be it so! I grant your wish.

## SCENE: 4

Gunadhya: According to scriptures, there was a time when the kings belonging to the Haihaya dynasty ruled the world. Most of them were merciless, and terrified the people. They disrespected the religious rituals and harassed the hermits. One such king was Karta-virya Arjuna.

Once he visited the hermitage of sage Jamadagni. Being the king of the land, the sage arranged a sumptuous feast for the king and his entourage. This not only pleased he king, but surprised him too.

Karta-virya: Sage! I am wonderstruck at the lavish feast you have arranged for me and my associates. From where have you got all this wealth?

Jamadagni: I did severe *tapasya* to propitiate gods. They were pleased to grant me a cow, Kamdhenu, which fulfilled all my needs. In fact, this celestial cow produces whatever object one asks for. Rajan! With the blessings of this cow, I have served you and your entire retinue to a royal feast.

Karta-virya: *Rishi*! Give this cow to me. My palace needs her more than your hermitage. In lieu of this cow, I will give you as much wealth as you want.

Jamadagni: Rajan! I cannot give this cow to you.

Gunadhya: The king got enraged. He asked his soldiers to forcibly take away the cow. At that very moment, Parashurama arrived at the *ashram.* When he saw the king misbehaving with

Jamadagni, and forcibly taking away the cow, he addressed his father thus:

Parashurama: Father! Why are you not confronting the king? You have all the yogic and spiritual powers to punish him.

Jamadagni: Son! The king is like the father of his subjects. His authority has to be respected.

Gunadhya: But Parashurama was made of different mettle. He could not tolerate the misconduct of Karta-virya Arjuna (a scion of the Haihaya clan) sliced his arms, and killed him. Then he went to the forest to meditate. Taking advantage of Parashurama's absence, Karta-virya's sons invaded Jamadagni's hermitage. They killed the sage. When Parashurama returned, he exacted vengeance for this evil deed.

Parashurama: I take a vow. I will clear the earth of the *Kshatriya* race.

Gunadhya: Parashurama travelled the whole earth and killed *Kshatriyas* 21 times, as his mother had beaten her breast 21 times when his father was killed. In fact, Parashurama indulged in genocide of *Kshatriyas*.

## EPILOGUE

After the massacre of Kshatriyas 21 times, Parashurama was advised "to go for penance to atone for the genocide." He donated the whole land he had won from *Kshatriyas* to sage Kashyapa, and moved to the forest to do *tapasya* to propitiate Lord Shiva. Eventually, Lord Shiva manifested himself to Parashurama and asked for his wish. Parashurama prayed to Shiva to restore his father to life. Lord Shiva was very much impressed by the *Bhakti* (devotion) of Parashurama, as well as for his adoration towards his father. Lord Shiva granted his wish and restored Jamadagni to life.

Since Lord Shiva was highly pleased with Parashurama, he blessed him with a wonderful *astra* (weapon), named *Bhargava-astra*. Hence onwards sage Parashurama came to be known as "Bhargava Rama." He continued to be an ardent devotee of Shiva. In the *Ramayna* when Rama breaks the *Shiv Dhanush* in the court of king Janaka, Parashurama suddenly appears on the scene. He is furious at the incident of breaking of *Shiv Dhanush*, and wants to punish the wrong-doer. Subsequently, he recognizes Rama as the incarnation of Lord Vishnu, cools down, and pays obeisance to him. This incident substantiates the dictum that Parashurama was a great devotee of Lord Shiva.

After being revived to life, sage Jamadagni continued with his austerities, and attained the higher status to be among the seven great sages, *Saptrishis*. According to the *Mahabharata*, it was *Rishi* Jamadagni who first introduced the *Shraddha* rites.

*****

# 14.RISHI PARASHU-RAMA: A SEQUEL TO SAGE JAMADAGNI

## DRAMATIS PERSONAE

GUNADHYA: The narrator

PARASHU-RAMA: A sage

JAMADAGNI: Parashu-rama's father

RENUKA: Mother of Parashu-rama

GANESHA: A deity

RAMA: Vishnu avatar

LAKSHMANA: Rama's younger brother

KARTA-VIRYA: King of Haihaya dynasty

# RISHI PARASHU-RAMA: A SEQUEL TO SAGE JAMADAGNI

## PROLOGUE

The Story of *Rishi* Parashu-rama is a sequel to the legend of his father, sage Jamadagni. They are interlinked. In fact, the stories of the father-son duo are supplementary to one another; one is incomplete without the other. And both the sages are equally renowned, are equally great. However, they are far different in their idiosyncrasies, in their individual natures. The father is, by and large, cool-headed; he generally remains calm and poised. But Parashu-rama's nature is notable for *krodha* (anger), violence, cycles of retaliation, the inappropriateness of *krodha* and repentance. However, Parashu-rama has different characteristic traits as compared to his father. He was an obedient son. He had a lot of respectful affection for his mother, Renuka. He was a staunch *Shiv-Bhakt* (a devotee of Lord Shiva). And he was a sage -warrior.

Parashu-rama literally means "Rama with an axe." He is the sixth avatar of Vishnu. He carried a number of traits which included aggression, warfare and valor, serenity, prudence, patience and repentance. His birth place is believed to be on the top of Janapav hills in Indore in Madhya Pradesh. On the top of the hills is a Shiva temple where Parashu-rama is believed to have worshipped Lord Shiva; the *ashram* is known as Jamadagni *Ashram*, named after his father.

## CURTAIN RAISER

My name is Gunadhya. I am a celestial being. I

came to the earth in the world of mortals as a story-teller. I was the narrator of tales in Somdeva's *Kathasaritasagara (KATHA-SARITA-SAGARA)*, that is the Ocean of Stories. And I am going to perform the same role of a narrator in telling the story of sage Parashu-rama.

The scriptures record that Parashu-rama was born to the Brahman sage Jamadagni and the princess Renuka, a member of the *Kshatriya* race. By his father's side, he descended from sage Bhrigu, and was the Bhargava. By his mother's side he belonged to the royal race of Kusikas. Saint Richika was his grand-father. And *Rishi* Vishwamitra was his *Mama* (maternal uncle). So, he hailed from an illustrious family.

Like other incarnations of Vishnu, he was foretold to appear at a time when overwhelming evil prevailed on the earth. The *Kshatriya* class, with weapons and powers, had begun to abuse their power, take what belonged to others by force and tyrannize people. Parashu-rama corrects the cosmic equilibrium by destroying these *Kshatriya* warriors. Rama cleared the earth of *Rakshas* (demons) like Ravana and his clan, and Lord Krishna annihilated the Kauravas and other sinners in the battle at Kurukshetra. Something similar was done by Parashu-rama to rid the earth of the *Kshatriyas* who committed all kinds of sins and atrocities.

## ACT: ONE

## SCENE: 1

Gunadhya: Sage Jamadagni, Parashu-rama's father, had a celestial cow, Kamdhenu, which gave all that the sage desired. A king named Karta-virya heard of the cow, and wanted to take it. But sage Jamadagni refused to part with the cow.

Karta-virya: Sage Jamadagni! I want this cow. Please give it to me.

Jamadagni: This divine cow has been gifted to me by gods. I would be committing a sin to part with a divine gift.

Gunadhya: King Karta-virya was not only arrogant but cruel also. Power and ego had gone into his head. He ordered his soldiers to tow the cow away. At that moment, Parashu-rama arrived in the hermitage. He got furious at the king's audacity, cut his hands and killed him. But his father, Jamadagni, was not pleased with this act of violence.

Jamadagni: Son! you have committed a crime. You should not have killed a king. This is a sin. You need to perform a penance to expiate for the crime. Please go away for a year and visit all the places of pilgrimage.

Gunadhya: Parashu-rama did what his father had ordered him. While Parashu-rama was away, the sons of Karta-virya attacked the hermitage, and killed Jamadagni. So angry was Parashu-rama at this dastardly act of the *Kshatriyas* that he killed all the *Kshatriyas* in the world with his axe (*parashu*). Twenty-one times, he rid the world of *Kshatriyas*.

## SCENE: 2

Gunadhya: Renuka, the wife of sage Jamadagni, one day, went to a river to fetch water. There she saw a Gandharva youth indulging in amorous dallying with a celestial nymph. The love scene animated love-desire in her mind for a fleeting moment. She no longer remained chaste of mind. When Jamadagni came to know of it, he lost the cool of his mind, and asked his eldest son to kill his mother for indulging in a sin. But he refused to obey the command of his father. Then he asked his other three sons, in order of birth, to behead their mother. But they too refused. This angered the sage. He cursed them and turned them into stones. Finally, he turned towards Parashu-rama, his youngest son. Ever obedient and righteous, Parashu-rama beheaded his mother with his axe. Then he approached his father.

Parashu-rama: Father! I have obeyed your command and killed my mother. I suffer from a sense of guilt. I want to expiate for the unrighteous act I have indulged in. I, therefore, submit myself before you to award me suitable punishment for the sinful act.

Jamadagni: Son! You have committed no sin. You were persuaded by your *pitri-bhakti* (devotion to your father) to behead your mother. I am highly pleased with your obedience. Please ask for the boon.

Parashu-rama: Please restore my mother to life sans any memory of what had happened to her; she be as chaste as before. And secondly free my brothers of the curse, and turn them from stones back to life. And please grant me the boon that I should be invincible in war.

Gunadhya: The purpose of this trial was to demonstrate the dharma of a son towards his father.

# SCENE: 3

Gunadhya: Parashu-rama, the sixth avatar of Vishnu, is one of the *chiranjeevis* (deathless) who has been present in all the *yugas*. He was present in the *Sat yuga*, *Treta* and *Dwapar*. And in the *Kali yuga*, he will be the guru of Vishnu's tenth avatar as *Kalki*. He is the only Vishnu avatar who is contemporary to Rama and Krishna in the *Ramayana* and the *Mahabharata* respectively.

Parashu-rama has been a staunch devotee of Lord Shiva. In fact, he was under the protection of Shiva, who instructed him in the use of arms, and gave him the *parashu* (the axe), after which he is named. The scriptures propound that once in *Sat yuga* Parashu - rama went to Kailash to pay his obeisance to Lord Shiva. Lord Shiva was asleep. Ganesha was guarding the inner apartments. He stopped Parashu-rama at the gate. A wrangle ensued.

Parashurama: Ganesha! How dare you block my way to Shiva!

Ganesha: My father is taking rest. Nobody can be allowed to meet him. You have to wait till he wakes up.

Gunadhya: The wrangle took an ugly turn; it erupted into a fight. Ganesha at first had the advantage. He seized Parashu-rama with his trunk, and gave him a twirl that left the sage senseless.

Parashu-rama: (*Soon recovering from the twirl*). I will cut your head off with my *parashu* (axe). *And then he threw his axe at Ganesha.*

Ganesha: I recognize this weapon as given to you

by my father. So, I refuse to counter this *parashu,* and receive it with all humility.

Gunadhya: The *parashu* fell on one of Ganesha's tusks, which it immediately severed. Since then, Ganesha has only one tusk, and is known by the name *Eka-danta* (single tusk).

## SCENE: 4

Gunadhya: Sage Parashu-rama was present in the *Treta Yuga* also. When Rama breaks the bow of Shiva (*Shiv-Dhanush*), he suddenly appears in the court of king Janaka. All the kings and princes present there, tremble with fear. He shouts:

Parashu-rama: Who has broken this *Shiv Dhanush*?

Rama: Sire! Only one of your *sevaks* (servants) can do this.

Gunadhya: And then follows a confrontation between two avatars of Vishnu, Parashu-rama and Rama. The wrangle becomes intense.

Parashu-rama: Rama! You say that you are my *sevak* (servant). But what you have done is the task of an adversary. You are my enemy. I should fight with you.

Gunadhya: Lakshmana could not tolerate the insult meted out to his elder brother. Annoyed by the rudeness and insolence of Parashu-rama, he accosted the sage.

Lakshmana: Sage! Why are you so furious about an old bow? In childhood we have broken so many bows of this type. This bow was so old and fragile that the mere touch of Raghunath Ji (Rama) broke it into pieces.

Parashu-rama: Lakshmana! You are just a child. Look at my *parashu*! It has killed many *Kshatriyas*. Mind your language, lest you should become a victim of my anger. Rama! Restrain your brother.

Gunadhya: Before the bitter exchange of words could turn into a bitter brawl, Rama intervened, and contained his younger brother. With all humility he played the role of a pacifist. Eventually, the verbal trial of strength ended in Parashu-rama's defeat.

## EPILOGUE

In the *Dwapar Yuga*, sage Parashu-rama played a significant role in the *Mahabharata* war also. He was the preceptor of Bhishma, Drona, Karna, the warriors who played an important role in the Great War. He also instructed Arjuna in the use of arms. It was Parashu-rama who gave Sudarshan Chakra to Krishna. He is also represented as being present at the great War Council of the Kaurava princes.

There is an interesting legend appertaining Karna as to how he became a disciple of Parashu-rama, and how the sage cursed him. Karna was actually the elder brother of the Pandavas. But his mother, Kunti, had concealed his birth for fear of social stigma. So, he was brought up by Adhiratha, the charioteer of king Dhrita-rashtra. Karna first approached guru Dronacharya, but he refused to make him his disciple, for he was deemed to be a low-born. Then he went to Parashu-rama and told him that he was a Brahman, and wanted to become his disciple to get instruction in the use of arms. One day Parashu-rama was sleeping with his head on the lap of Karna, when an insect crawled on him. The bite of the insect caused a lot of bleeding, but he sustained the stinging pain, and did not make any move, lest this should wake up his guru. When Parashu-rama woke up and saw Karna profusely bleeding, he visualized that his student had tricked him into believing that he was a Brahman, while actually he was a *Kshatriya*. This infuriated the sage, who cursed him that he would forget the *shastra-vidya* (use of weapons) at the time of dire need. It was this curse that eventually resulted in the death of Karna at the hands of Arjuna.

There was an intense fight between Parashu-rama and Bhishma at Kurukshetra over Amba, who was abducted by Bhishma, but refused to marry her. She did *tapasya* to propitiate Shiva, who granted her a boon that in the next birth she would become instrumental in the death of Bhishma. Amba was subsequently born as Shikhandi, who caused Bhishma's death at the hands of Arjuna.

There are legends dealing with the origin of the western coast geographically and culturally. It is believed that Parashu-rama retrieved the western coast from the sea, when he threw his battle *parashu* (axe) into the sea. As a result, the land of the western coast arose, and thus was reclaimed from the waters. In the present-day Goa (or Gomantak), which is a part of the Konkan, there is a temple in Canacona in the South Goa district, dedicated to Lord Parashu-rama.

*****

# 15. DHRUVA: HIS *TAPASYA* AND ASCENDANCE AS POLE STAR

## DRAMATIS PERSONAE

GUNADHYA: The Narrator

UTTANPADA: Son of Manu and father of Prahlad

SURUCHI: Elder wife of King Uttanpada, and mother of Prahlad

SUNITI: Younger wife of King Uttanpada, and step mother of Prahlad

PRAHLAD (DHRUVA): A devotee of Lord Vishnu, and son of King Uttanpada

LORD VISHNU: The Supreme God (*Jagdishwar*)

SEVEN SAGES: Marichi, Atri, Angira, Pulastya, Pulaha, Kratu, and Vasishta

NARAD: *Davarshi*, the divine seer

INDRA: Chief of the demigods

# DHRUVA: HIS *TAPASYA* AND ASCENDANCE AS POLE STAR

## PROLOGUE

*A scantily clad young man is seen standing with his face held high, and eyes glued to something up in the sky. He carries a tattered bag bearing some stories which seem to have been written thousands of years ago. In the background is a starry sky with "Dhruv Tara "(the Pole Star) becoming bigger and bigger than ever before with the time passing of. The man turns around, appears in all sagacity and smiling.*

According to the *Vishnu Purana*, the sons of Manu (*Swayam-bhuva*) were Priya-Vrata and Uttanpada. The latter had two wives, the favourite Suruchi, was proud and hauty; the second Suniti, was humble and gentle. The king doted on the younger queen, Suruchi; consequently, this fond endearment had made her presumptuous and arrogant.

Suruchi had a son, named Uttama. And Suniti too had a son named Dhruva. When Dhruva was just a child, he was berated and contemptuously treated by his step-mother Suruchi. Her hatred for Dhruva was born out of the fact that Suruchi wanted her son, Uttama, to succeed to the throne. Dhruva and his mother perforce yielded before this fait accompli.

## CURTAIN RAISER

My name is **Gunadhya**. I am actually a celestial being. I came to the earth in the world of mortals as a story- teller. I was the narrator of the tales in Somadeva's famous book, *Kathasaritasagara*

(*KATHA-SARITA-SAGARA*), that is the Ocean of Stories). And I am going to perform the same role of a narrator in telling the story of Dhruva. Before the all interesting and spiritually ennobling story of Dhruva (also popularly known as the "Pole Star") begins, I would like to dilate on the background of the Dhruva saga. Perhaps many people do not know the details of the famous socio-spiritual legend, which is steeped in rich religio-mythological annals, vis-a-vis his *tapasya* (penance) and his eventual ascendance into the heaven as a "pole Star." Dhruv was a descendant of Manu. The word Manu is from the root "man," that is to think, which literally means, the man with the faculty to think. Manu is believed to be *swayambhu*, that is self-existent, as identified with Brahma, the Lord of creation.

## ACT – ONE

## SCENE: 1

Dhruva: Mother dear! I want to go to meet my father.

Suniti: Please do not go there. You might be humiliated and embarrassed. Your tender heart will feel hurt.

Gunadhya: But Dhruva refused to be dissuaded notwithstanding his mother's warning. Persuaded by his love for his father, he ran to meet him in his chamber. There he saw Uttama (his step-brother and son of Suruchi) sitting in the lap of King Uttanapada. Dhruva also tried to sit in his father's lap.

Suruchi: (Suruchi shouted at Dhruva, dragged him from the lap of his father and rebuked him thus): Dhruva! You cannot sit there. If you want to sit in the King's lap you shall have to prove your worth by undergoing penance.

Gunadhya: Dhruva, protesting the ill-treatment meted out to him, remonstrated before his father.

Dhruva: Father! Why can't I sit in your lap like my younger brother?

Gunadhya: But King Uttanapada, afraid of Suruchi's anger, kept quiet. However, Suruchi intervened-

Suruchi: Arey Lalla! Without being born out of my womb, and being the son of some other woman, you cannot sit in the lap of the King. Your endeavour to fulfill your yearning is futile. If you want to sit in the King's lap, you shall have to prove your worthiness and undergo arduous tapasya (penance). You are a thoughtless simpleton. That is why you are craving for such a coveted position. It is correct that you too are a prince. But you are not my son. You were born of the womb of Suniti. Therefore, being the son of another woman, you have no right to sit on this throne. It is meant only for my son Uttama. As such, your despair is uncalled for.

Gunadhya: Thus, rebuked by his step-mother, Dhruva came back to his mother, crestfallen and morose. He obviously looked to be very angry.

Suniti: Son! What is the cause of your anger? Has anybody disrespected and denigrated you?

Gunadhya: Quivering in anger, Dhruva narrated the entire incident, the way his mother rebuked him, and the derision and disparagement he had suffered in front of his father.

Suniti: (*consoling and advising his son*): Son! what Suruchi has said is correct. You are unfortunate. Even the opponents could not have uttered such words of disparagement. But do not be disheartened and dispirited. Whatever you have done in your previous birth, who can alter that. And what you have not done, who can compensate you for that? Therefore, you should not feel annoyed at the words your step-mother has spoken. Men suffer or prosper depending on what they have done in their past lives. If one has done good deeds in his previous life, he becomes a king, has an umbrella held over his head, and rides excellent horses and elephants. Suruchi and Uttama must have done many good deeds in their previous lives, that is why they are better placed. Compared to them you and I might have done unethical and unrighteous deeds that we are in such a dire strait. I might have committed some sin in the previous life that I just remain the king's wife and not the queen in the real sense of the term. But son! I am not dispirited; for whatever God does is right. You and I should be satisfied with what we have. There is nothing to be unhappy about it. Verily, wise men are satisfied with what is ordained for them, they don't grumble. I know you are unhappy, my son, at what Suruchi, your step-mother, has said. But you should not take it to your heart; in fact, you should not bother at all. Instead, you should spend your time on being virtuous and religious, selfless, pious and pure. If you really feel hurt by the words of Suruchi, then you should imbibe in you result-oriented virtues which should do universal good. Just as the water flows towards the descent / slope, so do all riches, earthly and heavenly, flow towards the virtuous man, who follows the high road to humility and modesty.

Dhruva: Mother dear! I shall now try to attain the best and the most respected position. It is true that I am not the real son of Suruchi, but I would do such deeds as would make you proud of me. Uttama is my brother. I have no ill-will against him; In fact, I love him. Let my father give him the coveted throne. I don't desire it; nor do I need it. I am also not craving for any position or status given by someone else. I will now earn the position through my own virtuous actions, *tapasya* (penance) and exacting work.

## SCENE: 2

Gunadhya: Speaking thus to his mother, Dhruva went out of the palace. He eventually arrived at a lush-green forest. There he met seven sages (Rishi Marichi, Atri, Angira, Pulastya, Pulaha, Kratu, and Vasishta). Dhruva bowed in obeisance before the *rishis*, and spoke thus:

Dhruva: Reverend Sires! I am a son of King Uttanapada. My mother is Suniti. Filled with self-contempt, I have come to you for guidance.

Sages: Prince! You are just 5-year-old. We do not visualize any cause for your vexation, annoyance and irritation. Your father is still alive to take care of you. It also does not appear to us that you have lost something dear. Then what is the reason for your self-contempt and antipathy.

Gunadhya: Dhruva then narrated his story as to what had happened, and the bitter and contemptuous words his step-mother had spoken. Hearing his tale, the *rishis* wondered at the courage of the child, who obviously manifested the valor of a *kshatriya*.

Sages: Then what have you decided? Please tell us

about your intent. Also let us know as to what can we do for you? We visualize that you want to say something to us.

Dhruva: Respected sires! I have no desire for wealth, nor do I need any kingdom. I only want to attain that place where no one has so far reached. Honorable sires! the only assistance you can render is to guide me to the path which takes me to the highest position.

Marichi: Prince! Without Gobind's (Lord Krishna) worship man cannot attain that exalted state.

Atri: I tell you the truth. One who is able to please Lord Vishnu, he attains the highest position.

Angira: If you want to attain the first among- the-equal status, then worship *Janardhan*, (God Almighty).

Pulastya: One who worships *param-brahm* (the Supreme Lord) he achieves *moksha,* (deliverance).

Pulaha: By worshipping Lord Vishnu, Indra got the highest position among gods. You can also achieve that status by worshipping Lord Vishnu, who is the Master of the world.

Kratu: Lord Vishnu is *param-purush, yagyapurush.* He is *Yogeshwar.* When he is pleased, he can grant anything and everything, how-so-ever priceless it may be.

Vasishta: Dear son! By worshipping Lord Vishnu, you would get all that you wish, including the highest position in the *triloki* (the three worlds)

Dhruva: You have told me about Lord Vishnu whom I should worship. Please direct me to the course I should follow to please Him.

Sages: We give you the mantra that will lead you to Lord Vishnu. Please recite *"Om Namo Bhagavate Vasudeva."* By reciting this mantra, Manu, the ancestor of mankind, was granted all boons by Lord Vishnu. And you can also do so to please the Lord.

## SCENE: 3

Gunadhya: Having got the mantra and the advice, Dhruva left that place. He went to a place called Madhu situated in the deep forest. Since a devil named Madhu lived there, hence its nomenclature Madhuvan (Madhu forest). It was here that Madhu's son, Lavan, was killed by Shatrughan, Lord Rama's younger brother, who eventually set up a town there, called Madhura, which later came to be known as Mathura. Here Dhruva stayed put, and did arduous *tapasya*, and followed all the canons prescribed by the sages. His rigorous and harsh austerities unnerved Lord Indra. He consulted other gods, who too were worried by Dhruva's *tapasya*, and together they decided to disrupt Dhruva's penance. Since the gods wielded celestial power, they created an artificial Suniti, Dhruva's mother, who did her best to persuade Dhruva to break his *tapasya*, but to no effect. Dhruva remained steadfast and fixed in his penance, and did not falter from his course that he had charted out for himself. So much so that some devils frightened and terrified him, shouting "kill him, cut him into pieces, and eat him up." But nothing deterred the child, so immersed and absorbed was he in his devotion to Lord Vishnu.

When Dhruva was engrossed in penance, the divine sage *Devarishi* Narad appeared before him, and tried to dissuade him from undertaking severe austerities at such an early stage. Then an interesting interaction took place between *rishi* Narad, and Dhruva:

Narad: Dhruva! You are just a child. The forest is full of dangerous animals. How will you sustain the vagaries of the weather; the winter's cold and the summer's heat. Therefore, I advise you to abandon the idea of *tapasya* and go back home.

Dhruva: O learned sage! Even at the cost of my life, and all the rigors of the forest, I will do severe penance to please Lord Vishnu, and will thus prove myself worthy of sitting in the lap of my father.

Narad: Dhruva! I am astonished at your bold determination, which is unparalleled. Therefore, I will guide you towards your goal, and teach you all the rituals and mantras to meditate and to seek and please Lord Vishnu.

Gunadhya: Having been advised, Dhruva started his meditation, and went without food and water for almost six months. His mind was fixed in the Lord. The severe austerities unnerved the gods; they were caught by some unforeseen fear. Indra and other gods, then, decided to approach Lord Vishnu.

Indra: Supreme Lord! The demigods are scared of Dhruva's *tapasya*. As the moon waxes with every passing day, so does Dhruva; he is getting bigger and bigger and soaring high, day by day. Afraid of his stern penance, we have come to you with the request to help us tide over this problem. We fear that

Dhruva, through his penance, wants to usurp *Inderloka* (Heaven) and overthrow / supplaunt *surya* (the sun god), *Kuber* (the god of wealth), *Varuna* (the god of water, the sea god) and *Chandrama* (the moon god). Please help us get rid of this arduous problem.

Lord Vishnu: Listen gods! Dhruva has no desire for any status. Nor does he want to usurp the power and position of the Sun, the *Kuber*, the *Varuna*, or the Moon god. I know his wish, which I would fulfill. Please go back to your places, reassured that he has no intention to cause any harm to you. I am going to take care of that boy.

## SCENE: 4

Gunadhya: Having been assured thus, Lord Indra and other gods, bowed before Lord Vishnu, and returned to their respective places. And Lord Vishnu, pleased with the penance and devotion of Dhruva appeared before him.

Lord Vishnu: Dhruva, son of King Uttanapada! I wish you well. I am pleased with your *tapasya*. Ask for any boon.

Gunadhya: Dhruva heard the comforting words. But he would not open his eyes. Because he was still merged in his inner vision of Vishnu's form, as described by Narad to him. Lord Vishnu had to adopt a strategy of causing that inner vision to disappear. The Lord caressed his head with his hands. Dhruva opened his eyes, and seeing outside what he had been seeing all along in his mental vision, prostrated himself before the Lord. But Dhruva could not utter even a single word; his throat was choked by Lord

Vishnu's celestial manifestation. The Lord then touched his right cheek with his divine conch, which sparked off his speech.

Dhruva: (*He bowed before the Lord and paid obeisance to him*). Lord! If you are pleased with me, then I want to recite a prayer in your honour.

Gunadhya: Then from Dhruva's mouth outpoured forth a beautiful devotional hymn. He chanted prayers in manifold words, eulogized and glorified Lord Vishnu, and paid him reverence in twelve powerful verses, which together are called *Dhruva-stuti*.

Lord Vishnu: I am pleased with your devotion, my child! Tell me what do you want!

Dhruva: O Lord! Whatever I wanted; I have achieved. My penance has been successful; you have manifested yourself; I am delighted and gratified. I have had your full "darshan."

Lord Vishnu: But prince! My "darshan" never goes unrewarded. Therefore, demand whatever you want. Any boon you ask for, I will give it to you.

Dhruva: O, God! You are the Lord of the whole world. You reside inside my heart; so also, in the hearts of everybody. What I desire is not hidden from you. You know my Lord, what my step-mother had said in arrogance: "One who is not born of my womb, he is not fit to ascend the throne." Therefore, with your blessings my Lord I desire to occupy that highest place which is the prop of the entire world.

Lord Vishnu: Dear child! You had pleased me in your previous birth also. Therefore, I grant your wish: you will attain that place you desire. In the previous birth, you were a Brahmin, who was devoted to me, and who served his parents dutifully, and believed in the universal good. As time passed, a prince became your friend. He was very handsome, and enjoyed a life of opulence and luxury. Owing to his company and luxurious life, you harbored a desire that you should also become a prince. That is why you have been born in the family of Manu, and became a son of King Uttanapada. As such you already occupy a unique position. You have got which others cannot even think of.

My son! You will achieve that stature, that position which would be unparalleled and inimitable in the whole of the *triloki* (three worlds). You will become a star in the firmament. I give you that fixed position which is far superior to, and far above the Sun. the Moon, the *Mangal* (the Mars), the *Budh* (the Mercury), the *Brihaspati* (the Jupiter), the *Shukra* (the Venus), and the *Shani* (the Saturn) and the seven sages (*Sapt rishis*). Your position is fixed in the constellation where you will ever shine.

Gunadhya: Thus, Dhruva became the "DHRUV TARA," the "POLE STAR," round which circle the *saptrishis* (the seven sages).

## EPILOGUE

Dhruva was advised by Lord Vishnu to return to his kingdom. He dutifully followed the Lord's dispensation, and came back home. He was warmly received and welcomed by his family, including his step-mother, Suruchi, who regretted her past behavior and sought forgiveness. King Uttanapada abdicated the throne in favour of Dhruva, who was anointed as the king at the age of six. Dhruva ruled for many years with love in a just and fair manner.

Dhruva had achieved his goal. He had pleased Lord Vishnu through his penance. And even had the rare opportunity to see Lord's manifestation. God granted him a unique boon. There is no gainsaying the fact that Dhruva is remembered by all for his strong determination. Verily, one who has a strong determination, has his will. God graced Dhruva with an eternal status in the heavens. Even today we know him as the "DHRUVA TARA," that is the "POLE STAR."

Dhruva, the Pole Star, fixed in the northern sky, substantiates Dhruva's unique penance. The moral that we draw from Dhruva's story is that one who is steadfast in his determination, and is single-mindedly devoted to Lord Vishnu, he is bound to achieve his objective, and attain his goal. Dhruva's mind was replete with self-confidence. He was unwavering in his resolution, despite varied odds and hurdles. That is why he could make possible which was impossible.

*****

# 16. THE STORY OF PRAHLAD AND NARSIMHA AVATAR

## DRAMATIS PERSONAE

GUNADHYA: The Narrator

HARINYAKASHIPU: *Daityaraj* (the demon king)

PRAHLAD (DHRUVA): Son of Harinyakashipu

KAYADHU: Wife of Harinyakashipu

BRAHMA: Lord of Creation

INDRA: Chief of the gods

NARAD: *Devarshi*, a divine Rishi *Rishi*

SHUKRACHARYA: Guru of demons

SHAND AND AMARK: Sons of Shukracharya

VISHNU: The Supreme Lord

NARSIMHA: Half-man half-lion, an incarnation of Vishnu

TAKSHAK: Chief of snakes

PRIESTS: Brahmins

KRITYA: an ogress

BOYS: Students of the *Gurukul* (school)

A Guru

Tuskers

Cooks

# THE STORY OF PRAHLAD AND NARSIMHA AVATAR

## PROLOGUE

According to the *Vishnu Purana* and the *Bhagvad Purana*, there are interesting mythical annals behind the story of Prahlad and his father Harinyakashipu and uncle Harinyaksh.

The myth has it that once upon a time, several sages went to the *Vaikunthaloka* (the Heaven). This was the place where Lord Vishnu lived. The sages desired to see Vishnu Himself. However, they were stopped at the gate by two sentries who stood guard there, and would not let the *rishis* go in. This enraged the sages, who felt insulted. Consequently, they cursed the sentries that they would be thrown out of the Heaven, and would be born on the earth. These two sentries were named Jaya and Vijaya. Eventually, the two sentries were born as *asuras* (demons), and were named Hiranyaksh and Hiranyakashipu (they were twins).

In fact, Prahlad's story appertains Lord Vishnu's fourth avatar (incarnation) as *Varaha* (Boar). *Rishi* Kashyap had two sons. Hiranayakashipu and Hiranayaksh, and one daughter, Singhika. Singhika was married to Viprachitti. The story has it that Hiranyaksh, a demon, had dragged the earth into the bottom of the sea. In order to rescue the earth, Lord Vishnu assumed the form of a *Varaha* (Boar), and after a contest, he slew the demon Harinyaksh, and raised up the earth. This had antagonized Hiranyaksh's elder brother, Harinyakashsipu, who vowed to take revenge of his brother's death. He, thus, harbored a grudge against Vishnu, whom he wanted to punish. And for this purpose, he went to the Mandrachal Mountains, and there did *tapasya* (penance) for many years. The purpose of the penance was to equip himself with divine powers to take revenge on Vishnu.

## CURTAIN RAISER

My name is Gunadhya. I am actually a celestial being. I came to the earth in the world of mortals as a story-teller. I was the narrator of tales in Somdeva's famous book *Kathasaritasagara* (*Katha-sarita-sagara*), that is the Ocean of Stories. And I am going to perform the same role of a narrator in telling the story of Prahlad. It is an interesting tale of interaction between *bhakt* (devotee) and *Bhagwan* (God), between an adorer and devout and God's revelation in manifold acts. It is a socio-spiritual legend, dyed in rich religio-mythological flush. And it is a story of sin and its destruction, of evil and its annihilation.

## ACT: ONE

## SCENE: 1

Gunadhya: Hiranyakashipu undertook severe austerities, and after *tapasya* for many years, Lord Brahma was pleased and He manifested himself to him.

Brahma: Hiranyakashipu! I am pleased with your *tapasya*. I want to grant you a boon. Please let me know your wish.

Hiranyakashipu: (*Bowing his head in respect, and*

*with folded hands)* Please make me immortal.

Brahma: This is not possible. I cannot grant this boon, as it would disturb the system of the mortal world. Everybody who is born is destined to die. Therefore, ask for some other boon.

Hiranyakashipu: Sire! Then grant me the boon that I should not be killed of anything born from a living womb; nor be killed by a man, nor by an animal; neither during the day, nor in the night; neither indoors nor outdoors; neither on land, nor in the air, nor in water; and nor by any man-made weapon.

Brahma: (*Brahma had understood that his smart devotee had virtually asked for a boon for immortality. He ruminated over the fact that none became his bhakt (devotee). And if I do not grant the boons to Hiranayakash, he would dbecome my enemy):* After thoughtful consideration, he said *"Tathastu! Be* it so! Your wish is granted."

Gunadhya: The boon conferred upon Hiranyakashipu by Brahma made him invincible. Resultantly, he undertook a campaign to dominate the entire universe. He declared himself God Almighty. So great was his might that *devas* (demigods) constantly remained in awe of him. He lived in a magnificent palace made of crystal.

## SCENE: 2

Gunadhya: When Lord Indra found that Hiranyakashsipu had gone for *tapasya* (penance), he thought it as an opportune time to attack the demon - kingdom of Hiranyakashsipu. At the time of the great war between gods and demons, Prahlad's mother was pregnant. The demigods, led by Indra, defeated the *asuras* (demons), who ran helter-skelter in different directions and hid themselves. The victorious demigods eventually swept over the cities of the demon king, and ransacked them. Indra himself entered the palace of Hiranyakashipu, and forcefully captured Kayadhu, Hiranyakashipu's wife, and made off towards Amravati (Indra's kingdom). Kayadhu was very angry, and she reprimanded Indra.

Kayadhu: Indra! You are the king of gods. It does not behove you to kidnap someone else's wife. If you want your wellbeing, then leave a *pativrata* (faithful wife) forthwith, and send her back home. I beseech you to leave me; let me go!

Indra: No. I will not leave you. You are carrying a snake in your womb. I will kill your child as soon as he is born.

Gunadhya: The chastisement of Kayadhu reached the ears of *Devarshi* Narad. Her cries filled the heart of *Devarshi* with pity. He soon manifested himself, and accosted Indra and interposed.

Narad: Indra! What are you doing? Excited and roused by your victory over the demons, you presume to have become high and mighty. Consequently, you have abandoned moral and ethical conduct. Your misdemeanor does not do you any credit. Don't you know that it is an unpardonable sin to abduct somebody else's wife. Therefore, do not take her to your kingdom. It is not right, for she is chaste.

Indra: *Devarshi*! I am not doing anything wrong. Her husband is our enemy. She is carrying within her womb Harinayakashipu's son. I just want to keep her in custody until the child is born. We will snatch the child, and kill the successor of the *daitya (demon)* dynasty. I have no other motive.

Narad: (Smiling at the arguments of Indra). Indra! Perhaps you do not know that the child who is in Kayadhu's womb is *chiranjeevi* (to live long), blessed with longevity. She is carrying in her womb a great soul. Don't try to kill him. In fact, it is beyond your power to kill him. There is no reason to be worried about. He will cause no harm to demigods. Rather he will become an asset for your welfare. He will be a great devotee of Lord Vishnu.

Gunadhya: Acting on the advice of *Rishi* Narad, Indra abandoned his design. He released Queen Kayadhu and allowed her to go.

Kayadhu: I thank you *Devarshi* for coming to my rescue. I pay obeisance to you.

Narad: *Putri* (daughter)! Where would you go now? Your *daityapuri* (demon kingdom) has been devastated. Since you are just like my daughter, I advise you to come with me to my hermitage, and live there under my protection and care until your husband returns after *tapasya* (penance).

Kayadhu: *Devarshi*! I accept your proposal. I will go with you to your hermitage.

Gunadhya: During her sojourn in the hermitage, Kayadhu served *Rishi* Narad with utmost devotion. She would chant Lord Vishnu's name, and worship Him. Notwithstanding being the wife of a demon king, she lived a pious life like a devout. For the well-being of her son, yet to be born, she observed all austerities; even slept on the floor.

Addressing the unborn baby, Narad preached her daily, delivered religious and spiritual discourses, and narrated devotional tales. The aim was to prepare the child still in his mother's womb for a holy and religious life devoted to Lord Vishnu. This was the way the child would never forget the preaching received in the pre-natal stage. For Narad knew that the still-to-be born child would become a great *bhakt* of Lord Vishnu.

## SCENE: 3

Gunadhya: After the successful *tapasya* and granting of boons by Brahma, Hiranyakashipu returned to his kingdom. Not finding his wife at home, he made enquiries about her. He was told about what had happened to her; how demigods invaded *Daitypuri* and ransacked it, and how his wife, queen Kayadhu, was forcefully captured and abducted by Indra. He was also told that his wife now lived at the hermitage of *Devarshi* Narad. Hiranyakashipu straight away sauntered towards Narad's *ashram* (hermitage). There he met his pregnant wife.

Hiranyakashipu: *Devarshi*! I am extremely grateful to you for rescuing my wife from the clutches of Indra, and for giving shelter to her in your *ashram* (hermitage). Now I would take my wife back home to my palace.

Narad: *Daityaraj*! I would request you to let your wife stay at my hermitage till she gives birth to her son. She is like my daughter. I will take full care of her.

Kayadhu: *Swami* (husband)! *Devarishi* is right. He has cared for me like a father does for his daughter. I am extremely happy and comfortable here. Therefore, I request you to please agree to *Rishi* Narad's proposal, and let me live here till the birth of the child.

Hiranyakashipu: Well! I cannot say no to *Devarshi,* so obliged I am to him. I let you stay here as you wish.

Gunadhya: Hiranyakashipu returned to his kingdom. He collected all the demons, waged a war against demigods and defeated them lock stock and barrel. He dethroned Indra from his *Indraloka* (Heaven), usurped his throne and kingdom, and imprisoned him and other gods.

Hiranyakashipu, owing to the boons granted by Brahma and his victory over demigods, had become mighty powerful and arrogant. The unbridled power that he had acquired made him subjugate the *triloki* (the three worlds), including the *Indraloka.* He had declared himself to be God and asked the populace to worship him. He pronounced and asserted that he represented all gods He proclaimed that he was the Sun, the Moon; the *Vayu* (god of wind), *Kuber* (the god of wealth). *Varun* (god of water, the sea god), *Agni* (god of fire) and *Yamraj* (god of death). Fearing his waxing powers, the demigods had abandoned *swargaloka* (the Heaven), turned themselves into human beings and roamed here and there on the earth. Hiranyakashipu lived in his grand palace, and enjoyed the dance and music of *apsaras* (celestial women).

# SCENE: 4

Gunadhya: (Prahlad, the son of the demon king, came home during the vacations. He met his father Hiranyakashipyu who lifted him up and made him sit in his lap and asked.

Hiranyakashipu: Dear son! Whatever you have read and learnt so far, please tell me about that in detail.

Prahlad: Sure, dear father! Whatever is embedded in my heart and mind, I narrate that to you in brief. One who is without beginning, middle and end; One who is unborn, sans age and death; One who is the beginning and the end of the world, I bow before that Lord Vishnu, and pay obeisance to Him.

Gunadhya:  hearing his son speaking reverentially for Vishnu, *Daityaraj* Hiranyakashipu, got furious; his eyes became red with anger. He stared at Prahlad, and rebuked his Gurus -Shand and Amark -for stuffing the child's mind with such rubbish.

Hiranyakashipu.  (*Addressing the teachers*) You fools! What is this? You disobeyed me and imparted different education to my son in defiance of my diktat.

Guru: *Daityaraj*! Please don't be angry with us. Your son is not speaking about the education we imparted to him. We don't know from where he has learnt all this.

Hiranyakashipu: Son! Who has given you this education? Your *gurus* say that they did not teach anything like this to you, nor given any such discourse.

Prahlad: Father! Lord Vishnu who resides in everybody's heart, is the teacher and master of all. None else except Lord Vishnu can teach anything to anybody.

Hiranyakashipu: You blockhead! Who is that Vishnu? You have the impudence of repeatedly declaring Vishnu as *Jagdishwar* (God of the world).

Prahlad: Lord Vishnu is the originator and the creator of the entire world. He beggars description. He is the Supreme Lord; he cannot be described, nor can He be explained in words.

Hiranyakashipu: Idiot! In my presence who else can be called *Parmeshwar* (Supreme Lord)?

Prahlad: Dear father! Lord Vishnu, the Supreme Lord, is not only the creator and controller of you and I, but also of all the denizens of the *daitya* kingdom.

Hiranyakashipu: Who is that sinner who has entered his mind? Under whose influence he is speaking such irksome and unpalatable words? Take away this transgressor. He has committed a grave sin. I do not know who is that enemy of mine who has put such offensive ideas in his mind. Listen Shand and Amark! You are Prahlad's teachers, it is enjoined on you to give him the right kind of education as I desire.

## SCENE: 5

Gunadhya: Following the orders of Hiranyakashipu,

the demons escorted Prahlad back to the school. After many years of education, Hiranyakashipu again called his son.

Hiranyakashipu: Son! I hope you have now got proper education. Therefore, tell me about what you have learnt.

Prahlad: Let Lord Vishnu who is the Master of the entire universe be pleased.

Hiranyakashipu: This boy is a bad soul. He still persists with the old rut. He does not deserve to live. If he lives, he will cause tremendous harm to his family. For he has become like a blazing amber for his clan. Therefore, kill him.

Gunadhya: Hundreds of *daityas* (demons) armed with swords, cleavers and spears, swooped on Prahlad, hit him hard with their weapons, but in vain. They could cause him no harm, not even hurt him.

Prahlad: Father! Listen to me. I am a devotee of Vishnu. He is my protector. He lives in me. He also lives in you. He lives everywhere, even in the arms you and your demons carry. As Such, these arms cannot cause any harm to me.

Hiranykashipu: You fool! Stop worshipping Vishnu; He is my enemy. Stop being simpleton. Mend your ways.

Prahlad: Dear Father! One who only utters the name of Vishnu, he gets liberation from birth, age, death. And that eternal Lord lives in my heart; then who can cause me any harm? I fear none.

Hiranyakashipu: Throw him before the poisonous snakes! Let them bite him, and with their venom kill him.

Gunadhya: *Takshak* (name of a snake) and many other venomous snakes bit Prahlad. But they could cause him no harm. He escaped unscathed sans any injury; thanks to the blessings of Lord Vishnu.

Snakes: *Daityaraj*! Look at our condition, at our broken teeth, our painful hoods, our trembling bodies. We have failed even to cause a bruise on his body. Sorry! Give us some other work. We cannot kill him.

Hiranyakashipu: (*To his mighty tuskers*): Hey, you elephants! Kill this child who has been misled by my opponents, and has turned against me.

Gunadhya: Huge tuskers lifted Prahlad and threw him on the ground, and trampled upon him. But they too failed to cause any harm to the devotee of Lord Vishnu.

Elephants: Sorry king! we could not kill him. Look at our tusks; they are all broken. Our feet, in the process to trample him, have all become soar.

Prahlad: It is not owing to me that the tusks of the tuskers have broken. This is all due to Lord Vishnu, who is the destroyer of my sufferings and troubles, and who punishes the evil-doers, and my tormentors.

## SCENE: 6

Gunadhya: Irked by his attempts to kill Prahlad coming to naught, the demon king ordered that the boy be burnt alive. Horrified at the turn of events, the priests present there intervened.

Priests: *Daityaraj*! please calm yourself. Cool your mind. King! give us a chance to reform him. We shall impart such education to him that he will not only become respectful to you, but will become your devotee, and worship you as does the populace of your kingdom. *Daityaraj,* childhood is replete with all kinds of flaws. Therefore, don't lose your temper.

Hiranyakashipu: And if you too failed, then what!

Priests: If we fail to bring him round, then we will invoke *"Kritya"* (a ferocious ogress) who will kill him.

Gunadhya: Following the advice of the priests, Hiranyakashipu became calm and collected. Prahlad was then taken to the *Gurukul* (school) by the priests and his teachers, Shand and Amark. But at the school, Prahlad, instead of being taught by his teachers, started teaching the students about his faith and philosophy and Lord Vishnu.

## SCENE: 7

Prahlad: (*At school 5-year-old Prahlad would address his fellow-students thus*): My dear friends! It is the right time to worship Lord Vishnu. It is the time when we have to get out of the sense -- gratification, and material entanglement.

Boys: (*Not paying any heed to what Prahlad said, the boys would invariably say*): Let us play. We are only kids. We would learn about Lord Vishnu when we grow older.

Prahlad: I know that you want to play; you just want to get sense-- happiness. But we need to understand about the dearest and the most important thing in life. And that is to know and understand the Supreme Lord. He is in everybody's heart. It is He and He alone who can make us contented and happy. Let us only chant His name: *"Om namo bhagvate Vasudevay."*

Boys: (*Gradually the boys began to listen*) Prahlad! Please tell us from where did you get this excellent knowledge? You are like us, just 5-year-old. You never went out of the school. Therefore, it is not possible that you got this knowledge from outside. Our teachers have also not taught us anything like this. Please tell us who is that who taught you this education?

Prahlad: The answer to your question is simple. While still in the womb of my mother, I had learnt this knowledge from *Devarshi* Narad. The Vedic seer daily delivered a spiritual discourse to my mother. I had developed consciousness while still in the womb, heard all the spiritual sermons, and did not forget them. I would advise you that by cutting free of the material world, we can know what we are. "I am not the body; I am the eternal spirit / soul in it." And that eternal spirit, that immortal soul, has its origin in Lord Vishnu; the eternal soul is the essential part of God. Like me you should also put faith in the authority of *Devarishi* Narad, and chant the name of Lord Vishnu and worship Him. And if you do that you would derive the same benefit, the same blessings, as I have.

Gunadhya: The news of Prahlad's preaching

reached Hiranyakashipu. He summoned Prahlad's teachers and priests and reprimanded them.

Hiranyakashipu: Tell me! What is that nonsense you have been teaching Prahlad? I understand that other students of the *Gurukul* (school) are also chanting the name of Vishnu.

Shukracharya: *Daityraj* (Demon King). This boy is incorrigible. We have been left with no other alternative except to invoke *"kritya"* (an ogress) to kill him.

## SCENE: 8

Gunadhya: Shukracharya asked his sons, Shand and Amark, to invoke *"kritya."* They chanted mantras. *"Kritya"* appeared. Shukracharya directed the ogress to kill Prahlad. The ogress did her best, but failed to cause any harm to Prahlad. It was so ordained that once *"Kritya"* is invoked and produced, she would kill her target. And if she failed, she would kill someone else. And it so happened that when the ogress failed to kill Prahlad, she was so irked that she killed Shand and Amark, the sons of Shukracharya, the *daitya* (demons) Guru. This made Prahlad despondent. Mercy personified as he was, he invoked Lord Vishnu, and supplicated for bringing them back to life. Lord Vishnu acquiesced. Both Shand and Amark got back their lives.

Thus, thwarted in his attempts to kill Prahlad, Hiranyakashipu's fury waxed. He decided to use every heinous and ruthless device to exterminate Prahlad. He instructed the cooks to poison Prahlad's food.

Hiranyakashipu: Cooks! I order you to poison the food of Prahlad, and kill him. He is a wicked and deleterious son! He should not live.

Gunadhya: The cooks did as they were instructed; served poisonous food. But because Prahlad thought of God Vishnu, the poison had no effect on him.

Cooks: (*Seeing Prahlad digest the poison, the cooks rushed to the demon king*). King! We administered the deadliest poison, but your son absorbed it without any harm.

Hiranyakashipu: Priests! Hurry up! Produce "*Kritya*" (ogress) and kill him.

Priests: Hey son! You are born in the famous family, the lineage of which goes back to Brahma. Your father Hiranyakashipu is God himself. Therefore, stop worshipping any other God, and worship your father.

Prahlad: I agree that the roots of my family go back to *Rishi* Marichi. I am proud of it. My father is also brave and respectful. But what have I to do with all these ideas? I am immersed in God Vishnu. I believe that only Vishnu resides in the hearts of everybody. He is the Master of all.

Priests: We had saved you from the fire, thinking that you will recant your faith in Vishnu. We did not know that you are such an imbecile; a thick-skinned ignoramus. We are now left with no option except to invoke "*Kritya*"and be done with you.

Prahlad: By what means one is killed, or saved, is irrelevant. What is relevant are the actions, good or bad, which regulate and decide the fate of a man.

Gunadhya: The replies and arguments of Prahlad angered the priests. They chanted mantras and produced a huge ogress. The ogress was like the flames of fire. It dug up the earth with its feet. And attacked Prahlad with a huge *trishul* (trident). But the *trishul* struck Prahlad's chest and broke into many pieces. This frustrated the ogress and it turned around and began to attack the priests instead. The priests ran here and there, but were all killed by the demon. This made Prahlad very unhappy. He prayed to Lord Vishnu:

Prahlad: My Lord Vishnu, master of all the worlds, creator of the universe! Please restore these priests back to life.

## SCENE: 9

Gunadhya: After praying to God Vishnu, Prahlad touched the dead bodies of the priests, and this touch infused life into them, and they stood up alive. The priests were extremely grateful to Prhalad for this life-giving gesture. The priests then rushed to Harinyakashipu, and narrated the whole incident to him. Harinyakashipu then called his son, and asked him:

Harinyakashipu: Who gives you these powers?

Prahlad: These are not my powers. These are the powers of Vishnu. Those who worship Vishnu He protects them, and stands by them in weal and woe. One who causes pain to others, God Vishnu punishes him for his evil actions. Since I am a devotee of the Supreme Lord, I can have no physical and mental distress.

Gunadhya: The demon King who was unaccustomed to the slightest hint of insubordination, finally took hold of the boy, and dragged him to a nearby cliff. With uncontrollable fury he threw Prahlad into the abyss. However, all-pervading God Vishnu caught hold of his devotee and saved him from the intended destruction. Then Hiranyakashipu called Shambrasur, the most powerful and ferocious demon, and ordered him to kill Prahlad. Shambrasur used *maya* to create illusions around Prahlad. But Prahlad kept thinking of Vishnu. Then Vishnu's weapon, *Sudarshan chakra*, came and destroyed all the *maya* (illusion). He then ordered that Prahlad be drowned into the sea. At the bottom of the sea, the demons put boulders on Prahlad, so that he does not escape death. But Prahlad continued to chant the name of Vishnu. He moved his body left and right at the bottom of the sea, which made the entire earth shake. God Vishnu saved him from death. Singhika, the sister of Hiranayakashipu, had received a boon that the fire would not burn her. She told her brother that she would enter the fire with Prahlad in her lap, but what happened was otherwise. Singhika died in the fire, but Prahlad once again escaped death owing to Lord Vishnu's blessings.

## SCENE: 10

Gunadhya: Notwithstanding all out efforts made by the demon king, Prahlad could not be killed. Prahlad, chanting the name of Vishnu in meditation invariably remained unhurt.

Hiranyakashipu: (*Screaming*) Where do you get

your supernatural powers from?

Prahlad: From the same source as you do. I derive my power from Vishnu. So, do you.

Hiranyakashipu: You will chant "Vishnu, Vishnu"! Tell me where does your Vishnu live?

Prahlad: Everywhere! If you look through my eyes, you will see Him all around.

Hiranyakashipu: Then Vishnu will be residing in you too.

Prahlad: Yes! He is there inside me. He is there inside you too. He is there in everybody, everything, animate and inanimate.

Hiranyakashipu: Then Vishnu would also be in the sword I am holding in my hands.

Prahlad: Yes! He is there in this sword also. That is the belief of a devotee.

Hiranyakashipu: Please tell me! Does your Vishnu sit in this pillar also?

Prahlad: Vishnu is present in the sword, in the pillar, in all that exists in the universe.

Gunadhya: Harinayakashipu ordered his men to tie Prahlad to that pillar. The mighty demon
then drew back his sword, and struck a blow at the column. Just as his sword fell upon it, the pillar burst into thousand pieces, and with a roar that deafened the cosmos, leapt out a wonderful and strange being from within. This was Lord Narsimha, an avatar of

Lord Vishnu. Hiranyakashipu, the demon king, tried his utmost to escape. But Narsimha, half-man, half-lion, caught hold of him, dragged him towards the threshold. There he put the *Daityaraj* (demon king) on his thighs.

Hiranyakashipu: You cannot kill me. Lord Brahma has given me the boon that neither man nor animal can kill me.

Vishnu: Look! I am half-man and half-lion.

Hiranyakashipu: I can neither be killed in the day, nor in the night.

Vishnu: Look! This is neither day, nor night. It is twilight.

Hiranyakashipu: I can neither be killed inside, nor outside.

Vishnu: You are at the threshold; neither in nor out.

Hiranyakashipu: I can neither be killed on the land, nor in the air / sky.

Vishnu: You are on my thighs; neither on the earth, nor in the sky.

Hiranyakashipu: I cannot be killed by any man-made weapon.

Vishnu: I will kill you with my nails.

Gunadhya: After thus nullifying all of Hiranyakashipu's boons of virtual immortality, Lord Vishnu tore his belly with his nails. Narsimha roared angrily. The rage of Narsimha did not subside even after killing Hiranayakashsipu. He was still roaring. Lord Shiva, Lord Brahma, and even goddess Lakshmi, manifested themselves and appealed to God Narsimha, of course from a distance, as no one dared come near the angry God. Finally, Brahma sent Prahlad to pacify Narsimha. Fearlessly, Prahlad went close to God Narsimha, laid himself flat at his feet, and supplicated for calm. God Narsimha raised Prahlad, and embraced him.

Narsimha: O son Prahlad! You had to bear the sufferings for so long. Please forgive me. Seek some boon.

Prahlad: (*Prahlad felt overwhelmed. The God of the universe was standing before him, and was caressing his head. Prahlad bowed before the Lord and said*): Ytheou are my true God. If you wish to grant me a boon, then kindly bless me that no desire for anything may arise in my mind. O God! my father had always spoken against you. Please free him from the sin he has committed.

Narsimha: Your father has now become holy, free from all sins.

Gunadhya: God Narsimha then escorted Prahlad to the throne of his father and made him sit on it. He was anointed king of the demons. Lord God instructed Prahlad to always do good to others, follow the path of virtues, righteousness, and impeccable good conduct and serve the people well. After advising him thus, God Narsimha disappeared.

# EPILOGUE

The story of *bhakt* Prahlad and his evil-minded father, Harinyakashipu, a demon king (*daityaraj*) once again reiterates what Lord Krishna says in the *Gita*:

*Yada yada hi dharmasya glanirbhavti bharata*
*Abhyutthanam adharmasya tadatmanam srijamyahm*
*Paritranay sadhunam vinashay ch dushkritam*
*Dharmasansthaparthaya sambhawmi yuge yuge*
*(Gita 4.7 and 4.8)*

*Yada yada (whenever) hi (surely) dharmasya (righteousness) glani (downfall or decline) bhavti (takes place) Bharat (the Indians) abhyutthanam (gets precedence, or prominence) adharmasya (unrighteousness) tada (at that time) atmanam (myself) srijami ahm (I manifest myself). Paritranay (to rear, rally) sadhunam (pious people) vinashay (destroy) ch (and) dushkritram (sinner, wicked) dharm (righteousness) sansthanpnarthaya (establish) sambhavami (manifest) yuge yuge (from age to age)*

Whenever, O Bharat, Righteousness (*dharm*) wanes, and unrighteousness is rampant, I manifest myself (the Gita 4.7).

I manifest myself from age to age to defend the pious, destroy the wicked, and strengthen dharma (the Gita 4.8).

There is no denying the fact that Almighty Vishnu (Krishna, or Hari) creates Himself. It is the function of God as Vishnu, the Protector of the world to keep the world going on the lines of righteousness. He assumes birth to re-establish right when wrong prevails. The Supreme, though unborn and undying, becomes manifest in human embodiment to overthrow the forces of ignorance and selfishness.

The dictum aforementioned is the crux of the saga of Prahlad and his devotion to Lord Vishnu who takes birth as Narsimha – half-man, half-lion – to punish the wicked and protect the pious and the righteous people.

Lord Krishna in the Gita reiterates the same precept in Chapter 10, verse 30:

*Prahladakshami daitynam kalah kalayatamahm*
*Mriganan mrigandro -ham ch vainateyashch*
*pakshinam*

*Prahlad ch (also) asmi (I am) daityanam (demons) kalah (time) kalyatam (among the destroyers) aham (I) mriganam (among animals) ch (also) vaintaya (Garuda) ch (also) pakshinam (among birds).*

***I am Prahlada among Titans, unit of time for calculators, the lion (mrigendr) among beasts, and Garud among birds.***

Even the names of the characters are highly significant. Look at Hiranyakashipu. "Hiranya" means soft bed, and "Kashipu" means gold. These were the basic principles of the life of the *Daityaraj* (the demon king). On the other hand, the Narsimha avatar (incarnation) has meaningful connotation. The word "narsimha"is derived from the Sanskrit word "nara", meaning man, and "simha" meaning lion. Thus, the Lord took the form of a part man, and part lion, to kill Hiranyakashipu, who otherwise could not have been killed by an ordinary man as he was granted boons of almost immortality by Lord Brahma. Further, Vishnu is traced from the root "vis", that is to enter into *prakriti*. In order to rid the world of the forces of evil and sin, ignorance and wicked oppressions, Vishnu takes *avatar* and descends and enters the earthly plane.

Similarly, Krishna is from the root "krish", which means to scrape, because He scrapes, or draws away all sins and other sources of evil from his devotees.

Even Singhika, the sister of Hiranyakashipu, has a great socio-cultural and religious importance. Since centuries she is known by the name of Holika. Hiranyakashipu was told that his sister, Singhika, has got a boon that fire cannot burn her. Therefore, she enters the burning fire with Prahlad in her lap. But Prahlad escapes unhurt, while Singhika is burnt to ashes, owing to the misuse of the boon granted to her. Thus, the festival of Holi is celebrated in memory and honour of Prahlad, who was a blessed soul. On the eve of the festival of colours, bonfire is lit in every nook and corner of the country to mark the destruction of the evil and unrighteousness, and the protection of the righteous, pious and the noble souls.

*****

# 17.YUDHISHTRA IN ELECTION FRAY: FROM MAHABHARATA TO BHARATA

## DRAMATIS PEROSNAE

GUNADHYA: The Narrator

YUDHISHTRA: The eldest son of Pandu, who appears in the

*Mahabharata* as "Dharamraja"

DURYODHANA: King Dhritrashtra's son

YAKSHA: A celestial being in the *Mahabharata*

NAHUSHA: The python king

President of the Screening Committee

Secretary of the Screening Committee

# YUDHISHTRA IN ELECTION FRAY: FROM *MAHABHARATA* TO BHARATA

## PROLOGUE

The philosophy of life after death draws its sustenance from the *Gita* and the *Upanishads*. For example, Lord Krishna in the *Gita* propounds: "You and I, Arjuna, have lived many lives. I remember them all. You do not remember "(*Gita*: 4-5). And "just as a person casts off worn-out garments and puts on others that are new, even so does the embodied soul cast off worn-out bodies and take on others that are new." (*Gita*: 2.22).

*Vasansi jirnani yatha vihaya,*
*Navani grihnati naro parani*
*Tatha srirani vihaya jirnani*
*Anyani samyati navani dehi*

*Vasansi (garments) jirnani (worn out) yatha (just as) vihaya (discards), navani (new clothes) grihnati (gets) nara (man) aprani (other) tatha (like this) shrirani (body) vihaya (discards) jirnani (old age) anyani (different) samyati (receives, gets) navani (new) dehi (body).*

(Like a man who puts on new garments after discarding his worn-out clothes, the embodied Self also casts off tattered bodies and transmigrates into other bodies that are new).

The *Rig Veda* also abounds in such references: "When after death all the five elements dissolve among themselves, the *jivatma* (individual soul) remains, and this *Jivatma* takes to itself a new body." (5.6). Even the Bible raises the same question: "If a man dies, will he live again?" (*Book of Job, Old Testament*: 2).

Going by the aforementioned dictum of the holy scriptures, let us imagine that the Pandavas brothers have re-emerged from the eons of the hoary past at Indraprastha. And that they are advised by Lord Krishna, and persuaded by Balrama to contest the elections to put the democracy of their Bharat back on rails. Lord Krishna suggests that let Yudhishtra try his luck at the hustings, for he has the experience of being an administrator, since he has been a king in the past. So, Yudhishtra, before he approaches the Election Committee with his bio-data, rehearses many times over the unforeseen interview before Krishna.

## CURTAIN RAISER

My name is Gunadhya. I am actually a celestial being. I came to the earth in the world of mortals as a story-teller. I was the narrator of the tales in Somdeva's famous book *Kathasaritasagara (KATHA-SARITA-SAGARA),* that is the Ocean of Stories. And I am going to perform the same role of a narrator in telling the story of Dharamraj Yudhishtra, supposing that he is reborn, and decides to contest elections in the present-day Indraprastha (that is Bharat). Duryodhana too is imagined to have been born in the present age, and he too tries to test his luck in the elections.

However, Yudhishtra is ignorant of the consequences he would be confronted with. There is no gainsaying the fact that the Pandavas would find the present-day socio-cultural and political scenario far different from that of the *Mahabharata* era.

They would be appalled and dismayed to know that the politicians in the present day Bharata have become specialists in the art of veiling, deceiving and cheating. Even if they dissemble to speak the truth, the common populace does not believe them. Because the politicians now-a-days say the nastiest things in the nicest way.

## ACT: ONE

## SCENE: 1

Gunadhya: Outside a tall, mansion-like building, all white and majestic, have gathered a large number of people, all accoutered in white khadi, donning jackets of motley colours, blue, brown, pink and yellow. Inside a room are seated in the chairs round a big table some senior leaders of a political party, comprising the Election Panel. Their faces are recognizable.

On the walls of the spacious room are hung life-size portraits of Mahatma Gandhi and Jawahar Lal Nehru. They manifest a smile of hope. On the right-hand corner, silhouetted in the background, there is a bronze statue with three monkeys, one refusing to see, the other adamant not to hear, and the third determined not to speak. But the leaders have turned their backs towards them. They are obviously oblivious of them. They are sifting through a pile of papers, which look like applications and bio-data of the prospective candidates aspiring to contest elections.

In the porch outside the room are sitting the ticket-seekers. Among them, sitting on a bench, is

Yudhishtra. He is empty-handed, with just a paper, perhaps his bio-data, protruding out of his pocket. On the other side of the row of benches, is seated Duryodhana. He has a brief-case resting upon his lap. His face reflects a gleam of confidence, and a glimmer of a politician well-versed in the art of hypocrisy and dissembling.

After a prolonged discussion and mutual susurrus, the Election Panel decides in unison to interview the prospective candidates. Yudhishtra is the first to be called. Then ensues an interesting question-answer session.

President: (*Yudhishtra enters the committee room. With folded hands he respectfully bows his head and greets the members. As we know him from the Mahabharata era, this gesture, a part of his characteristic attributes, was obviously expected of him. Pointing towards the chair, the President signals Yudhishtra to sit*). What is your name? Yes! It is there in the application. Yudhishtra! Well, Mr Yudhishtra! Please tell us what is your popular base? We have gone through your bio-data, this vital fact is nowhere mentioned.

Yudhishtra: Sire! I am a follower of righteousness. I am known by the nickname *'Dharamraja,'* not only in Indraprastha but also in the whole of the Aryavrata.

President: (*Smiling at the quaint reply, the president of the Election Panel further asks*) Not Dharam. I want to know your popular base vis-à-vis your caste and clan. How many of them are the voters in Indraprastha?

Yudhishtra: Sire! We are five brothers; each a paragon of virtue and valour.

President: Only five! That is your muscle power!

Yudhishtra: Sire! you don't know their prowess. Arjun is the best archer in the whole of Aryavrat. Bhim personifies great power and strength, unparalleled in the whole world. This is my muscle power unmatched even in the best of warriors.

President: Are you referring to that Arjuna who disguised himself as Brihanla, and clapped like a eunuch to save his life. Many Brihanlas have already become members of our party, and even won elections. That is no merit to garner votes. And about Bhima, less said the better. He disguised himself as a cook, and maintained a façade of dissembling to hoodwink.

However, tell us! In order to protect Arjuna, will your mother succeed in procuring *kawach* (protecting gear) and *kundle* (ear-rings) of Karna, even in the coming electoral battle?

Further, do you have any glamorous woman to attract electorates in the election campaign? Do you have some such tale that may fetch you sympathy votes?

Yudhishtra: Sire! We have Draupaddi, wife of five brothers. Her *cheer-haran* (disrobing) by Duryodhana and Dushasan would be made an issue to secure sympathy votes. (*However, Yudhishtra turned a deaf ear to the Karna's Kawach and Kundal question*).

President: Draupadi! One wife of five brothers. What kind of *dharam* is this Dharamraj! We want a *kulvadhu* (virtuous woman of a noble family) and not a *nagarvadhu* (a courtesan). And at the time of *cheer-haran*, all the five brothers, warriors great, by whom you so often swear, they sat quiet with their heads down, and did not protest, not even engender confidence by way of making a statement of condemnation. You could not make an issue then. How would you make an issue now after so many centuries!

Even otherwise clothes are no longer an issue these days. Many scantily clad women are already members of our party, and even have been elected as legislators. Therefore, for our party *cheer-haran* could not be an election issue. Tell us some other vote-garnering issue.

Yudhishtra: The great Bhisham Pitamah, Kakashri Vidur, Kulguru Kripacharya, and Guru Dronacharya, have all extended their moral support to us. They are certainly big names to impress and influence the electorates.

President: This is electoral Mahabharata, and not a platform for discourse on *nitishastra* (ethics). We want active participation of the popular leaders in the election campaign. All these big names are of no use to us in the elections. Those who gave you only moral support in the battle with the Kauravas, will not serve any electoral purpose now. Our party in the elections does not need any moral support, but actual and active support.

Yudhishtra: *Disheartened Yudhishtra played the last 'chal' (move) on the 'chauser (dice-board)*: Sire!

We have the blessings of Lord Krishna.

President: (*Bursting into a horse laugh, the President, in the tone of an opinionated person, said*): Son! you are ignorant about the present-day political situation and social reality. Today, the political issue is not Krishna. It is Rama. When you get the blessings of Rama, then come to us for the ticket. In that eventually, we may consider your application favourably. We are sorry! You don't fit in the electoral strategy of our party.

## SCENE: 2

Gunadhya: The Secretary of the Screening Committee then rang the bell, and asked the peon to call in Duryodhana.

Prince Duryodhana walks in the Committee Room with his usual mannerism: vanity, boast and pretension personified. Before the President of the Election Panel asks Duryodhana to sit down in the chair, Duryodhana literally throws his brief case -- which he was carrying -- on the table with a bang.

President: (*Surprised, the President asks*): "Son! what is this?"

Duryodhana: (*He straightens himself, displays a winning smile on his face, and erupts into a peal of laughter. Clearing his throat, he replies in his heavy voice*): Sire! here are 500 gold coins for the party. Accept my contribution.

Gunadhya: (*The members of the Election Committee, looked at each other with gleeful smile, they rolled their eyes here and there, nodded their heads in appreciation, beckoned the peon, and with a wave of hand indicated to him to take the brief case inside).* Then thus they proceeded with the interview.

President: Duryodhana! History has it that Indraprastha was ruled by the Pandavas, and not by the Kauravas. We don't think, you, as the Kaurava chieftain, made any mark, politically, socially and culturally, and created any popular base.

Duryodhana: *(Duryodhana raises his eyebrows, and asks in his usual garrulous voice):* Base! What is that thing? *(And himself answers the point):* Elections are not won on the basis of any base, but with money and muscle power. And I have both of them. In the Indraprastha constituency, there are not as many polling booths as the number of my brothers. I have one hundred brothers. If one brother 'manages,' yes 'manages', one polling booth, yet several of my brothers will still remain surplus.

President: Duryodhana! How many musclemen do you have?

Duryodhana: Do you think one hundred are less? Each of my brother is a wrestler. Then I have many other princes, progenies of those kings and potentates who had helped us in the Mahabharata War. Besides that, Karna, the great archer, is my all-weather friend.

President: But son! Karna is famous for his charity! That is why he is called "Danveer Karan." If Mata Kunti once again seeks his *kawach* (protecting gear) and *kundal* (ear -rings), then you are sure to lose the whole battle, the way you lost in the Mahabharata War.

Duryodhana: (*Waving his heavy mace in the air*) Gone are those days. Times are different now. The idiosyncrasies of the people have undergone a complete metamorphosis, as also the priorities. Karan has become wiser, more sagacious. Karan will not commit the mistake he committed during the Great War. He has learnt a lot from his past experience. Yet, in the eventuality Mata Kunti insists on *kawach* and *kundal*, then we have the Gafar Market. Karan can buy a duplicate *kawach* and *Kundal* and give it to his unwary and credulous mother.

Gunadhya: The members of the Committee were taken aback at the audacity and ready-wit of Duryodhana, and the confidence his face exuberated. The Secretary looked towards the President, and spoke in a hush-hush voice in his ears.

Secretary: "Sir, he is a useful man!

President: (*The President shook his head in approval*): Yes! this is true that you have a lot of muscle power with which you will succeed in bogus voting, as also in booth capturing. But to succeed as a politician, one needs to have strategy, political philosophy and a bit of diplomacy. Do you have any person, who, like a statesman, has these qualities, essential for winning an election?

Gunadhya: Duryodhana heaved a long sigh. With a mischievous glint in his eyes and a Machiavellian smile on his face, he pitied the lack of common sense of the Committee members. He blurts out:

Duryodhana: Sire! don't you know that Shakuni is

not only my maternal uncle, but also my mentor, philosopher and guide! And in the entire Aryavrat, there is no bigger strategist and intriguer than Shakuni. (*Caressing his long whiskers with his fingers, he further adds*): You must know that "uncle Shakuni, when he rubs *pasas* (pawns) of the *chausar* (dice board) in his hands, then many a stalwart remain awe-struck at the excellent throw on the dice. He is such a person who can manipulate defeat into victory, *alpmat* {minority) into *bahumat* (majority). History has it that he has won many an electoral battle through his machinations. Uncle Shakuni will be my Election Manager.

President: But Duryodhana, you disrobed Draupadi. If the opposition makes it an electoral issue, then not only your election, but the election of the entire Aryavrat, will be jeopardized.

Duryodhana: (*Raising his eyebrows like a big bully, he shamelessly points out):* Sire! who cares for the incident of disrobing now-a-days? It could not become an issue then, when the incident happened in the distant past; how will it become an issue now! The common populace has a very short memory. Moreover, incidents of disrobing of women happen day in and day out these days, and no longer become any news. Nor do such incidents remain in the news for long in the print and electronic media. Therefore, disrobing of Draupadi will neither be an issue, nor any news, in the coming elections.

President: But you are notorious as a criminal, as a goon, as a terrorizing bully. And as such owing to your criminal background, your nomination is likely to be challenged by your rivals, and in that eventuality, it is likely to be cancelled by the

Election Commission.

Duryodhana: What nonsense! Who dares give evidence against me? And when there is no evidence, there is no case, and as such there is no crime. (*Before the President could ask the next question*), Duryodhana asserts: Listen to me Mr. President! Tatshri Bhishm Pitamah will campaign for me. And when he campaigns and supports me, the entire Aryavrat will fall in line.

Secretary: (*At this point of the interview, the Secretary of the Election Panel, intervenes*). But the moral support of Bhisham Pitamah is with the Pandavas. Besides, he is lying on the bed of arrows, how would he campaign for you?

Duryodhana: (*Duryodhana, dissembling seriousness like a seasoned and well-groomed politician, points out*) Bhisham Pitamah had taken a vow, and given a word to his father that he would be loyal to the Hastinapur throne. And since I am a prince of Hastinapur, therefore, he is bound by his vow to support me. Further we will politically exploit Pitamah's lying on the bed of arrows, waiting for death. Since Pitamah was made to lie supine on the bed of arrows by Arjuna, we would make that an issue, propagate it and garner sympathy votes. And we have another plus point. The great Sanjay, bestowed with the divine eyes by *Rishi* Ved Vyas, who narrated the *Mahabharata* story live to my father, King Dhritrashtra, will do the necessary election propaganda in my favour.

President: But Sanjay was an official communicator, a King's broad-caster. How can he be a campaigner of an individual?

Duryodhana: What is official about it! I will manipulate everything. I will find a way and hoodwink the Election Commission.

Gunadhya: *The members of the Election Committee, then, go into a huddle, discuss the electoral prospects of Duryodhana among themselves. After that the President announces the result.*

President: "Son! We are not only fully satisfied with your interview, but also pleased with you. You have all the virtues of a leader, and qualities of a successful politician. Therefore, we have decided to recommend your name to the High Command to give you the party ticket to contest election from the Indraparstha Constituency. May God bless you!

## SCENE: 3

### *(Yudhishtra From Mahabharata to Bharata)*

Gunadhya: According to the mythical history, Yudhishtra personifies righteousness; he epitomizes truth and virtue and ethical qualities. As such, Yudhishtra of the Mahabharata continues to follow his characteristic qualities even in the modern Bharata. He has not changed. He remains immutable. Consequently, Yudhishtra of the historical past finds himself a misfit, a failure, in the present-day socio-political and cultural ambience. On the other hand, Duryodhana who represents unrighteousness, remains as unscrupulous and unprincipled even in the present times as he was during the Mahabharata era. Therefore, he finds himself acceptable in the present-day socio-political atmosphere.

Interestingly, Yudhishtra who had answered all the questions of the Yaksha in the *Mahabharata*, and had ultimately succeeded in bringing his dead brothers back to life, failed to give satisfactory answers to the questions of the lesser mortals, and thus appeared to be insufficient in getting the ticket for contesting the election. Not only that, he even gets a severe drubbing at the hands of the members of the Election Panel. He is unable to convince them about his uprightness and virtues.

We know the story of the riddle-contest between Yudhishtra and the Yaksha that appears in the *Vana Parva* of the *Mahabharata*. The story appertains an incident when the Pandavas end their twelve years of exile in the forest. In the thirteenth year the Pandavas were supposed to live in *agyat vas* (living incognito). It so happened that one day, while roaming in the forest, Yudhishtera became exhausted and thirsty. He asked his brother Nakula to fetch water. Nakula found a beautiful lake. When he attempted to take water from the lake, there came a voice from the void: "O Nakula, the water of this lake will turn into poison if you take it without answering my questions." Nakula did not pay heed to the warning, and hurriedly took water from the lake and drank it. Nakula died instantly.

When Nakula did not return for long, Yudhishtra sent his twin Sahdeva in search of his brother. He too reached the same lake, and was similarly warned. But he too drank the water and died. In the same manner, both valiant Arjuna and powerful Bhima, met the similar fate.

Since none of the brothers returned with water,

Yudhishtra embarked on their search. He followed the same path, and eventually reached the same lake, where he found his brothers lying dead. Before searching for the killer of his brothers, he decided to quench his thirst. And then came the same voice. The sagacious Yudhishtra understood the turn of events. He agreed to answer the questions put forth by the invisible voice. Thus, began the question-answer dialogue between the Yaksha and Yudhishtra:

Yaksha: Who makes the sun rise and ascend in the skies, and who moves the sun around? Who makes the sunset in the horizons?

Yudhishtra: Brahma makes the sun rise and ascend. The gods perambulate about the sun, and the Dharma sets the sun.

Yaksha: What instills 'divinity' in Brahmins? What is the quality of virtuosity in a Brahmin, and what is the human -like quality of a Brahmin?

Yudhishtra: The self-study (*swadhyana*) of the *Vedas* is divinity in a Brahmin. Penance is the quality like a virtuous person, and death is human-like quality in a Brahmin.

Yaksha: What instills divinity in *Kshatriyas*, and what is the quality of virtuosity in a *Kshatriya*? And what is the conduct like a non-virtuous person in a *Kshatriya*?

Yudhishtra: The art of archery instills divinity in a *Kshatriyas*. Oblation is the quality of virtuosity in a *Kshatriya*, while fear is his humanity. And if a *Kshatriya* abandons people under his protection, then his conduct would be akin to that of a non-virtuous person.

Yaksha: What is heavier than the earth, higher than the heavens, faster than the wind and more in numbers than the straws?

Yudhishtra: One's mother is heavier than the Earth: one's father is higher than the heavens; the mind is faster than the wind, and our worries are more in numbers than the straws.

Yaksha: Who is the friend of a traveler, and who is the friend of one who is ill, and one who is dying?

Yudhishtra: The friend of a traveler is his companion: the physician is the friend of one who is sick, and the charity is the friend of a dying man.

Yaksha: What is that which when renounced, makes one lovable, and what is that which when renounced makes one happy and wealthy?

Yudhishtra: Pride, if renounced, makes one lovable; desire, if renounced, makes one healthy, and one who renounces avarice, obtains happiness.

Yaksha: What enemy is invincible? What constitutes an incurable disease? Who is noble and who is ignoble?

Yudhishtra: Anger is the invincible enemy. Covetousness is a disease that is incurable. He is noble who desires the well-being of all creatures, and one who lacks mercy is ignoble.

Gunadhya: Yudhishtra had answered all the questions of the Yaksha. The Yaksha was so pleased with Yudhishtra that at the end of the questions, he revealed his true identity as *Yama-Dharma*, the god of death, and restored all his brothers to life.

## SCENE: 4

Gunadhya: Further, in the *Mahabharata* (*Vana Parva*), Yudhishtra has an encounter with a huge python. The python is, in fact, king Nahusha, one of the ancestors of the Pandavas. Nahusha, through a long penance, had acquired the throne of Heaven. This made him so arrogant that he forgot the distinction between *dharma* and *adharma,* that is between righteousness and unrighteousness. Many great *Rishis* bore the car of Nahusha through the air. One day it so happened that he touched with his foot the great sage Agastya, who was carrying him, on his head. The sage in his anger cursed Nahusha: "Fall, thou serpent," and Nahusha fell from his glorious car and turned into a python. Agastya, at the supplication of Nahusha, put a limit to the curse. Consequently, Nahusha had been waiting for eons for the instrumentality of Yudhishtra for a discourse on *dharma.*

The story has it that one day Nahusha (python) got hold of Bhima. He was about to crush him when Yudhishtra came there in search of his brother. He pleaded for the release of Bhima. Nahusha said that he would let his brother go, if he answered his questions on *dharma.* Yudhishtra agreed. Then ensued the following question-answer discourse between Nahusha and Yudhishtra:

Nahusha: What made a Brahmin, Brahmin?

Yudhishtra: Virtues like truthfulness, generosity,

forgiveness, goodness, compassion, self-control, etc. constituted a Brahmin.

Nahusha:   The qualities and virtues that you mention go against the principle of four *varnas* (four castes). For even a *sudra* (low caste) may have all these virtues. Virtues
Cannot be the he monopoly of any caste.

Yudhishtra: Indeed, if a *sudra* is characterized by all these virtues, he is to be 'defined' as a Brahmin. And if a Brahmin lacks these qualities, then he is to be regarded as a *sudra*.

*Gunadhya:* The discourse ended Nahusha's curse. He threw off his huge reptile form, became clothed in a celestial body, and ascended to the heaven.

## EPILOGUE

There is no gainsaying the fact that Yudhishtra of the *Mahabharata*, manifests his dexterity to satisfy both the Yaksha and Nahusha with his equitable and righteous answers. But the same Yudhishtra fails to answer the questions in the manner and to the extent expected of him by the members of the Election Committee. The reasons are not far to seek.

Webster's Dictionary defines two types of politicians. One who is experienced in the art and science of government, and the other who is primarily interested in political gains and narrow selfish interests. We have lost down the decades the politician of the first type. It is the second type of politician who rules the roost, who has downgraded democracy as the government 'off' the people, 'far' the people and 'buy' or 'bye' (good bye) the people.

Yudhishtra belongs to the political class of the first type, and Duryodhana to the politics of the second kind which connotes that politics these days has become symptomatic of the game of scheming, cunning, hiding, veiling, hypocrisy, crime, lies, manipulation and self-aggrandizement. Shakespeare nicknames such politicians as "scurvy politicians", obviously a speaking sobriquet. The new political class is different from their predecessors, qua the politicians of the past era. That is why Yudhishtra is a failure in the given socio-political ambience, for he remains steadfast in his characteristic idiosyncrasies, and has not changed with the passage of time. Hence the journey of Yudhishtra is from Mahabharata to Bharata, from success to failure.

*****

# ABOUT THE BOOK

**KNOW THE SEERS OF INDIA** provides a deep insight into the life and relevance of some of the most significant Rishi*s,* who founded the Hindu community. There is no gainsaying the fact that the Hindus are *Rishi Santan* (progeny of sages). The seers, qua the sages, of ancient India are our ancestors, our forefathers. The lineage of each Hindu family goes back to one or the other *Rishi*. This fact stands substantiated by sub-castes and surnames, such as Bharadwaja, Kashyap, Parashar, Vashisht, and so on. And so are the *Gotras* named after different *Rishis*. The sub-castes, as also *Gotras*, named after renowned *Rishis*, accentuate and endorse the dictum that the Hindus all over the globe are the descendants of the sages.

As a *Rig Vedic* term, *Gotra* simply means "cow pen," or "herd pf cows." The specific meaning being "family lineage kin" (as it were herd within an enclosure). No socio-religious ritual, or rite, such as marriage, child-birth, *mundan, Shraddha* rites, is complete without invoking the *Gotra* of the family. Verily, sub-castes and *Gotras* identify us with the past, with the *Rishis* of India. This book condenses information for all who are in search of their past, their roots, their identity.

# ABOUT THE AUTHOR

Dr. C. D. Verma is a former Associate Professor, and Head, Department of English, Hans Raj College, a premier institution of Delhi university. During his four decades of long teaching career, he has written a number of books and articles. His articles have been published in leading magazines, newspapers and research journals. His books, the *Gita in World Literature, the Exile Hero and the Reintegrating Vision, W. H. Auden (Selected Poems) Look Back in Anger* and *Mrs. Dalloway (Sterling Publishers)* have been widely acclaimed. His latest books, *The Sermons in Stones (Untold legends of Temples and Towns, and Socio-Cultural Stories),* and *Something to Crow About (A collection of Short Stories and Parables)* have been published by Amazon.